Gifting Right

BY

LESLIE SORG

CCC PUBLICATIONS • LOS ANGELES

Published by

CCC Publications
20306 Tau Place
Chatsworth, CA 91311

Copyright © 1990 Leslie Sorg

All rights reserved by CCC Publications. No part of this book may be reproduced or transmitted in any form or by any means, electronic or mechanical, including photocopying, recording or by any information storage and retrieval system, without the written permission of the publisher, except where permitted by law. For information address: Mark Chutick/ CCC Publications; 20306 Tau Place; Chatsworth, CA 91311.

Manufactured in the United States of America

Cover design © 1990 CCC Publications

Cover Production by The Creative Place, Woodland Hills, CA.

Cover background wrapping paper by Jillson & Roberts Gift Wrappings, Inc.; Irvine, CA.

ISBN: 0-918259-24-X

If your local U.S. bookstore is out of stock, copies of this book may be obtained by mailing check or money order for $4.95 per book (plus $1.50 to cover sales tax, postage and handling) to: CCC Publications; 20306 Tau Place; Chatsworth, CA 91311.

Pre-publication edition—2/90

TABLE OF CONTENTS

THE CONCEPT

INTRODUCING THE CONCEPT..........................1

ONE

THE GIFT MESSAGE 4
What Message Does Your Gift Send?..................4
The Four Kinds of Gifts That Focus The Message..5
    Practical 6
    Decorative 7
    Durable 8
    Emotional.. 9
Knowing Your Message Means Success............10

TWO

APPLYING THE CONCEPT................................11
Categories To Make Future Choices Easy........11
Direct Yourself To Where The Best Gift Is.......11
Example Gift Ideas For Each Category.............13
    Appliances... 14
    Beauty Products 15
    Clothes.. 16
    Clothes Accessories 17
    Comfort 18
    Cultural/Entertainment 19

Den/Office.. 20
Educational... 21
Exercise/Fitness.. 22
Food/Beverages... 23
Gadgets 24
Hobby/Interests 25
Home Furnishings/Decorative 26
Home—Outdoors 27
Kitchenware... 28
Leisure/Outdoors.. 29
Serving Pieces.. 30
Sports 31
Stocking Stuffers—Big & Small...................... 32
Travel... 33

THREE

THE EASY WAY TO PROFILE GIFT RECIPIENTS..34

The Five Age Groups For Gift Giving 34
Children 35
Teenagers.. 35
Adults-Acquiring.. 36
Adults-Established 36
Seniors... 36

Your Relationship With The Giftee...................37
Close Friends.. 37
Casual Friends/Acquaintances...................... 37
Office/Work Colleagues 37

Specific Profile Questions **38**
    About Interests 38
    Lifestyle Tastes That Refine Gift Choices 38

Wrap-Up **39**

FOUR

THE OCCASIONS **40**

Define Occasions & Discover Ideas
   Automatically **40**
    Annual Holidays, Birthdays 40
    Anniversaries 41
    Weddings 41
    Second Weddings 42
    Wedding Showers 42
    Baby Showers 43
    Host/Hostess 44
    New Home, House Warming 44
    Get Well 44
    Just Because 45
    Office Occasions 45
                Birthday 45
                Holidays 45
                Retirements/Leaving an
                organization 46
                Tokens upon return from
                vacations/trips 46

THE ENHANCERS
FIVE

Ideas That Enhance Any Gift............................48
    Enhancer #1:   Add Visual Texture &
                                     Color Contrasts.................. 48
    Enhancer #2:   For More Texture, Add
                                       The Unexpected.................. 49

Creative Gift Combinations............................49
    Enhancer #3:   Add A Contrasting Gift........ 50
    Enhancer #4:   Contrast Gift
                                       Purposes 50
    Enhancer #5:   Theme Gifts........................ 51
                                       How To Create Themes 51
                                       More Examples of Gifts &
                                       Themes 51
    Enhancer #6:   Add-ons.............................. 54
                                       How To Expand 22 Office-
                                     Related Products To
                                     Hundreds of Gift Ideas........ 54
    Enhancer #7:   Present Everyday Items
                                       in Quantity........................ 62

Examples of Combination Gifts 63
Summary 66

THE ORGANIZERS

SIX

KEEPING TRACK THE EASY WAY......................67

Remembering Gift Ideas..................................67

    Tracking Idea #1: Write Down Clues As Soon As You Recognize Them!................... 67

    Tracking Idea #2: Incorporate Gift Ideas Into Present Recordkeeping System........ 69

    Tracking Idea #3: For More Elaborate Recordkeeping—An Easier Way.......................... 69

    Tracking Idea #4: Remembering Dates — Only 12 Cards..................... 72

    Tracking Idea #5: Know Your Gift Giving Needs For An Entire Year & Other Organization Tips....................................... 73

Summary..74

SEVEN

TEN EXTRA TIPS THAT WRAP IT UP................76

v

THE LISTS

EIGHT

GENERIC GIFTS..80

34 Items That Adapt To Any Person, Occasion Or Budget......................................80

NINE

GIFT SOURCES TO USE NEAR HOME OR FAR AWAY..94

Overlooked Sources..94
- Hardware stores..................94
- Book shops.........................94
- Office supply stores............94
- Sporting goods shops..........95
- Toy stores...........................95
- Gift, novelty and card shops.................................95
- Artists' studios....................95
- Public libraries...................96
- Magazines/newspapers advertisements...................96

Institutions, sites or products indigenous to a city, country or region..............................96
- Museum shops....................97
- Special exhibits..................97
- Local products....................98
- Special celebrations............98
- Hometown nostalgia...........98

Using Everyday Lists For Ideas.........................99

Services are Gifts Too! 100

TEN

FOR THE PERSON WHO HAS EVERYTHING
.... 102

ELEVEN

GIFTS ON A TIGHT BUDGET 105
Low or No Cost Gifts 105
   Your Time 105
   How To Present Intangible Gifts 107
   Tangible Gifts 107
How to Stretch Your Dollar 113

TWELVE

A 1001 GIFT IDEAS — MASTERING YOUR GIFT SEARCH 116
Examples of Gift Choices 117
PRACTICAL GIFTS 125
   For Children 125
   For Teenagers 125
   For Acquiring Adults 126
   For Established Adults 128
   For Seniors 130
   For Acquaintances 131
   For Office Colleagues 133
   For Friends 134
   For Birthday/Annual 136

    For Office.. 138
    For Host/Hostess.. 139
    For Housewarming 140
    For Wedding Showers 141
    For Weddings... 142
    For Second Weddings... 142
    For Baby Showers... 144
    For Anniversaries.. 144

DECORATIVE GIFTS...**146**
    For Children 146
    For Teenagers... 146
    For Acquiring Adults... 146
    For Established Adults 148
    For Seniors.. 149
    For Acquaintances.. 150
    For Office Colleagues 151
    For Friends/Relatives... 151
    For Birthday/Annual... 152
    For Office Occasions 153
    For Get Well... 154
    For Host/Hostess.. 154
    For Housewarming 155
    For Wedding Shower.. 156
    For Weddings... 156
    For Second Weddings... 157
    For Baby Shower 158
    For Anniversaries.. 158

DURABLE GIFTS **160**
    For Children 160

    For Teenagers 160
    For Acquiring Adults 160
    For Established Adults 161
    For Seniors 162
    For Acquaintances 163
    For Office Colleagues 164
    For Friends/Relatives 164
    For Birthday Gifts 165
    For Office Gifts 166
    For Get Well Gifts 166
    For Host/Hostess Gifts 167
    For Housewarming Gifts 167
    For Wedding Shower Gifts 168
    For Wedding Gifts 169
    For Second Wedding Gifts 169
    For Baby Shower Gifts 170
    For Anniversary Gifts 170

EMOTIONAL/FUN GIFTS 172
    For Children 172
    For Teenagers 172
    For Acquiring Adults 173
    For Established Adults 175
    For Seniors 176
    For Acquaintances 177
    For Office Colleagues 178
    For Friends 179
    For Birthdays 181
    For Office Occasions 183
    For Get Well 184

ix

For Host/Hostess 185
For Housewarming 186
For Wedding Showers 187
For Weddings 188
For Second Weddings 189
For Baby Showers 190
For Anniversaries 190

FOR PERSONS WITH EVERYTHING 192

THE CONCEPT

INTRODUCING THE CONCEPT

Imagine yourself selecting wonderful gifts *every time* for your spouse, your children, your relatives, your boss, or your best friend. No matter how many gifts you present these special people over the years they'll be pleased. Now imagine you can do it quickly, easily, and without anxiety. Would you like to learn a foolproof method to quickly decide upon and select the best gift for each person on your gift list, and to do it right every time? Then, this book is for you.

This book has plenty of gift ideas, but it offers more than that. It shows you **how** to choose gifts.

Gifting Right was developed to help you find the best gift for any person, for any occasion and within any budget. This new method gets you results every time and without anxiety.

To master the Gifting Right method requires a new way of thinking. When you put it into action, your gift selections will give both you and the recipients satisfaction and pleasure.

It doesn't matter whether you are looking for a wedding gift for a friend, a birthday gift for your mother, a "get well" gift for your boss or an "I'm sorry" gift for your spouse.

The concepts are generic and thereby apply to everyone. The **Gifting Right** method explains what to get, why it is the most appropriate choice and how to make it more creative or personalized.

The **Gifting Right** approach is broken down into four parts: the **concept**, the **enhancers**, the **organizers** and the **lists**.

THE CONCEPT

The **Gifting Right** concept explains the message of giving and the four gift categories that will direct you to the right gift every time. You will learn a more effective way to look at the recipients in assessing their gift needs or desires. After reading this section you will never look at gift giving the same way. The facts are so basic that you will wonder why no one has revealed them previously. They will make your approach to gift choosing quick and easy. You can apply these common sense methods to every person or situation, whatever your budget and wherever you live.

THE ENHANCERS

The enhancers are practical and creative tips that can be applied to every gift to make it more personalized and complete. This section shows how to make any gift a little more special.

THE ORGANIZERS

The third section provides suggestions for remembering important dates and organizing your gift giving needs for an entire year in advance. It concludes with overall tips to put your mind at ease at gift giving time.

THE LISTS

The last part of the book includes dozens of lists which can be used to brainstorm any time you wish. The lists also reinforce the vital facts you learned in the first section of this book. Used together, you should never again have a mental block or experience frustration in selecting gifts.

* * * * *

As you incorporate the **Gifting Right** way of thinking into your life, you will never panic again when choosing gifts. Eventually, you will be able to quickly choose successful gifts even when this book is not handy.

The Concept

However, if the book is not handy, there is another tool to aid you in this common sense and easy approach. The last page of this book is a *tear-out* which can be folded in quarters to a convenient wallet size. It contains capsulated key facts and lists from **Gifting Right**. After reading **Gifting Right,** a glance at the page will help you come up with the best gift ideas quickly. Your mental blocks and previous frustration in choosing gifts will be over.

Now, you're on your way.

ONE

THE GIFT MESSAGE

What Message Does Your Gift Send?

Every gift sends a message whether you intend it to do so or not. The message doesn't necessarily have anything to do with the cost of the gift. It primarily has to do with how *appropriate* the gift is. And this is accomplished by matching the gift with a person's interests, desires and lifestyle. If you remember this fundamental principle, you will already be well on your way to **Gifting Right** every time.

Let's imagine you suddenly remember that you need to send a birthday present to your twelve-year-old nephew. You race down to the local toy store, select a big expensive game, and mail it off while congratulating yourself on getting one more chore quickly out of the way. You will probably never hear it from your relatives, but when your nephew received the gift from you he was heartbroken. Why? Because (1) you obviously didn't remember when you visited last Christmas that he received a similar game and expressed his dislike of games; (2) you didn't include a personal note or birthday card; and, (3) you totally forgot that he'd been hinting all year that he would really love for you to take him with you on your next weekend fishing trip.

Although you got him a substantial gift, what message did you send him without meaning to? You told him you were too busy to think or really care very much about the life of your twelve-year-old nephew. Think how ecstatic your nephew would have been on the other hand, if you had presented him with a hand written *certificate* that was "good for one fishing trip with your uncle" because he always expressed delight in hearing your fishing stories and often hinted about going fishing with you!

Later in the book you will learn other ways to personalize gifts. For example, taking the boy fishing is a "service" gift, not a "product" gift, and in this case, much more effective. But the

The Concept

message is the first and most important thing to remember in selecting a gift. You should always ask yourself,, **"What is the message I want to send?"**

> I love you
> I'm thinking of you
> I think you're great
> I'm happy for you
> I'm sorry
> I'm proud of you
> You are important to me
> etc.

The Four Kinds of Gifts That Focus The Message

You are making rapid progress. First, you know who you are selecting a gift for (the Giftee) and what underlying message you want to send to the Giftee through the gift. Next, you must decide which of the four basic categories or kinds of gifts you wish to give. Understanding and selecting gifts from these choices will not only keep you close to the gift message, **but will cut your gift selection time in half!**

The four categories that all gifts fall within are:

Practical

Decorative

Durable

Emotional

Some gifts may fall into more than one of the four categories listed above; and, you may select more than one gift for a very special person, so that you give him or her something from each of the four categories. Therefore, the next thing to ask yourself after you have determined the message you wish to send is, **"What shall the primary function or purpose of my gift be?"**

It is amazing to think that four simple categories could aid your gift giving searches so effectively. But they do. These four categories will eliminate an enormous amount of confusion.

Once again, remember that the four categories of gifts are:

PRACTICAL

DECORATIVE

DURABLE

EMOTIONAL

You should review these four categories before you select a gift. By choosing a gift purpose immediately your search will be more focused. By reviewing your chosen purpose *after* you have decided on a gift in relation to all four gift categories, you can ensure that its final selection and presentation is complete. You will be "completing" your gift message. The latter concept is discussed in Chapter 5, "The Enhancers."

The easiest way to understand these categories is to give examples:

PRACTICAL

When a gift is "practical" it is functional and less frivolous.

Practical	**Non-Practical**
Drinking glasses	Balloons
Toothbrush	Rubber duck for tub

Perfume—
    For a date
	Perfume—
	    for a swimming party

Business book	Racy novel

THE CONCEPT

(Continued)	
Practical	**Non-Practical**
Unadorned sunglasses	Sunglasses with animals and flowers glued on
Seeds for a flower garden	Fresh cut flowers
Helping a friend hoe and and plant the seeds	Taking a friend for a drink (when neither of you has "a problem to talk out")

DECORATIVE

A gift will be decorative according to your visual interests and styles, and to how you apply them to the Giftee. As you will see, "decorative" can apply to food and personal use items as well as traditional decorative items for the home.

Decorative	**Non-Decorative**
French pastries	Loaf of bread
Box of fancy steak knives	Paring knife
Bed linens	Bed pillow (no pillowcase)
Hair ribbon	Bobby pins
Man's tie	Collar stays
Outdoor candle lantern	Flashlight

DURABLE

If you want something to *last* for many years, you can give a vase, or pen, computer software or a photograph. But if the gift only needs to *last* a few days, you can give fresh flowers or a favorite candy. "Durability" is how you define it.

In terms of selecting gifts, you need to understand what makes a gift "durable." What length of time makes a gift durable? What length of time will satisfy your "durable" need for a particular gift. Consider among your choices how long the *thought* of the gift stays with the Giftee, not only how long a tangible product will last.

Here is a sample of time frames that show how an item(s) can adapt as a durable gift whether it lasts a day or a lifetime.

1	day	Romantic evening (but one's memory can last forever)
1	week	Fresh cut flowers (which is why they are extravagant)
1	month	Potted flowers
1-2	years	Magazine subscriptions , auto accessories, posters
10	years	Kitchen appliances, glasses
20	years	Paintings, prints, decorative accessories like candlesticks, wastebaskets, china, dishes, framed mirrors, vases
Forever		Jewelry

Here are specific durable vs. non-durable gift examples that show you how certain gifts can have a "durable" quality, depending how you view it and how it is contrasted with other items:

The Concept

Durable	Non-Durable
Bottle of brandy (consumed slowly)	Bottle of everyday wine (consumed in one sitting)
Potted plant	Cut flowers
Magazine subscription for one year	One issue of magazine
Reference book	Best seller (fiction)
Swiss Army knife	Plastic picnic knives
Bicycle	Certificate for bike tune-up
Aged cheese	Fresh fruit
Joke book (that can be repeatedly read over the years	Joke book (with dated jokes, usually read once and passed on to a friend)
Season tickets to cultural or sports event	A pair of tickets to one event

EMOTIONAL

Emotional gifts constitute any gift that will evoke an emotional response—either a warm smile, laughter or a heartfelt tear. An emotional gift can be decorative, practical or durable, but it can also stand on its own. It can be totally frivolous or quite serious. It can also be extravagant, or with no use whatsoever.

In fact, every successful gift will be emotional to some extent. In the **Gifting Right** method, the emotional category is used when a gift needs to fill the emotional purpose *most of all*.

Emotional	Non-emotional
Flowers	Vase
Candles & bath oils	A lamp*
Lingerie	Flannel nightgown
Personalized tie-tack	Man's tie
Nostalgic photographs	A photo album
A video of your favorite movie	Membership at a video rental store
Personalized dog bowl for a beloved pet	Dog leash
Coupon for 3 massages	Coupon for exercise classes

*Occasionally, even the most mundane article can become an "emotional" gift if there is an incident or memory between the gift giver and Giftee. For example, if you and your spouse broke a lamp during your honeymoon, a lamp may evoke warm and loving, or humorous memories. Under normal circumstances, a lamp would be considered non-emotional.

Knowing Your Message Means Success

As you can see, your gift search will be easier, more enjoyable, and more successful, if you keep in mind the *message you want to send*, and *choose the best purpose among the four kinds of gifts*—decorative, practical, durable and emotional. Remember that your gift will reflect a personal message from you to the Giftee, so modify the definitions to suit your situation.

The concept of these four categories is really simple. Read on for more time-saving and fun ideas...

TWO

APPLYING THE CONCEPT

Categories To Make Future Choices Easy

Have you ever wondered if there was an easy way to sort through all the gift choices out there? How does one make the best selection from among the thousands of wonderful gift ideas bombarding us daily in stores, catalogs, advertisements, magazines and other gift books? How does one sort through these ideas quickly?

It probably seems that if there were fewer choices, the gift selection process would be easier. You're right.

To aid you, I have researched every type of gift. I discovered that 20 generic categories cover virtually every type of product or service you would give as a gift.

Direct Yourself To Where The Best Gift Is

Next time you're not sure what gift to get, glance at these 20 categories and pick one or two that seem appropriate for the specific person and occasion.

By choosing one of the 20 categories, you will be able to direct yourself to the most appropriate store or catalog. Then, once situated in the correct "department", you can be "inspired" by the latest products and select the best, most appropriate gift.

Manufacturers, advertisers and retailers are constantly working to come up with better products and more creative presentation. You just need to know how to eliminate the choices that are not right for you, so you can concentrate on the best gift ideas in the correct category. (Of course, having first selected one of the four gift purposes, this next step will be a quick and easy task.)

Why agonize, when you can let the creative ideas of merchandise marketers lead you to wonderful gifts? Just get yourself to the right location.

Now, the categories:
- Appliances
- Beauty products
- Clothes
- Clothing accessories
- Comfort
- Cultural/entertainment
- Den/office
- Educational
- Exercise/fitness
- Food, beverages
- Gadgets
- Hobby/special interests
- Home furnishings/decorative
- Home gifts for outdoors
- Kitchenware
- Leisure/outdoors
- Serving pieces, for entertaining (eating/drinking)
- Sports
- Stocking stuffers
- Travel

Let's say you were planning to get a female friend a birthday gift. A quick profile of your friend might look like this: She is a career woman; likes a variety of sports; and, is meticulous about her appearance, but is not a "clothes horse." Sounds like a practical lady which means you can play it safe and get her something practical. But, to make her feel she is getting a "gift" (something she wouldn't buy or do for herself), help her splurge.

Look at the 20 categories. You will see that a few categories are much better for her than others. What categories would be personal splurges for her? Entertainment? Get her tickets to a show. Comfort? Find or make her a lap blanket. Clothes? How about a sweater for her "after work" hours? Now, you're getting the message!

The Concept

Example Gift Ideas For Each Category

What follows are numerous gift ideas from the previous categories. Glance at the category headings first. If one or more appeal to you for a specific person's gift, look at the ideas listed under that heading. If either the heading or gift suggestion hits a chord, you will know that you should go to a store or use a catalog that would have those types of items.

The lists are not meant to be all-inclusive, but they will give you plenty of general and specific items. Use the pages of this book as your personal reference guide. Write in your own gift ideas, as well as stores or catalogs you do not want to forget.

APPLIANCES
Think about each room in one's house; and what appliances are used—around the house, outdoors or for hobbies.

Easy reference—Your list of stores/catalogs:

Sears Roebuck	Best
Montgomery Ward	Lillian Vernon
J.C. Penney	Service Merchandise
K-Mart	
Target	
Builders Emporium	

- Camera
- Ceiling fan
- Coffee maker
- Electric appliances—clock radio, electric razor, telephone answering machine
- Electric saw
- Fire extinguisher
- Flashlight
- Hair appliances
- Humidifier
- Iron and board
- Kitchen appliances—electric knife, can opener, food blender, juicer
- Popcorn maker
- Portable stereo/radio
- Radio
- Tape cassette
- Telephone
- TV
- Vacuum cleaner
- VCR
- Waffle iron

THE CONCEPT

BEAUTY PRODUCTS
Whatever makes a man or woman feel or look more attractive—head to toe, inside and out

Easy reference—Your list of stores/catalogs:

Macy's	_____
Nordstrom's	_____
Nieman-Marcus	_____
Elizabeth Arden	_____
Broadway	_____
Local beauty suppy shops	_____

    Color charting—personalized up to $100, or a book on selecting better colors for you and your wardrobe
    Facial
    Hair accessories
    Make up brushes
    Manicures, Pedicures
    Teeth, newly capped or bonded
    Tinted contact lens
    Vitamins

CLOTHES
For men, women, or children—for day, night, work or play?

Easy reference—Your list of stores/catalogs:

Nordstrom's	L.L. Bean (1-800-221-4221)
Saks Fifth Avenue	Spiegel Catalog
Nieman-Marcus	J. Crew Catalog (1-800-562-0258)
Sears-Roebuck	Adam York
Broadway	The Limited

- Dress
- Jacket
- Lingerie
- Pajamas
- Robe
- Shirt
- Slacks
- Socks
- Sweater

The Concept

CLOTHES ACCESSORIES
Consider what accessories are used head to toe—head, neck, shoulders, arms, wrists, fingers, waist, legs, feet

Easy reference—Your list of stores/catalogs:

Saks Fifth Ave.	Horchow Collection
Nordstrom's	
Broadway	
Antique Clothing Stores	
The Limited	

- Belt
- Blazer buttons
- Evening bag
- Gloves
- Handbag
- Hat
- Jewelry
- Scarf
- Shoe trees
- Slippers
- Suspenders
- Stockings
- Wallet
- Wristwatch

COMFORT

Anything that makes a person more comfortable physically, mentally or emotionally, or feel decadently entrenched in luxury

Easy reference—Your list of stores/catalogs:

_____	Comfortably Yours Catalog
_____	Brookstone Catalog _____
_____	_____
_____	_____
_____	_____

Bed tray
Blanket for bed, car, picnic or football stadium
Facial
Massage
An outing with you—bring friends to a favorite restaurant, park, tennis club or movie
Pedicure, manicure
Remote control button for lights, TV
Limousine ride to/from anywhere

The Concept

CULTURAL/ENTERTAINMENT
At the theater, exhibit, or home

Easy reference—Your list of stores/catalogs:

Museum/theater gift shops _____

Smithsonian _____

Metropolitan Museum of Art _____

Museum of Modern Art _____

Local zoo _____

_____

- Museum membership
- Opera glasses
- Theater tickets
- Movie coupons
- Five gallons of popcorn
- Phonograph records
- Tape cassette
- Compact disc
- Video cassettes, blank or movies for rent

GIFTING RIGHT

DEN/OFFICE
Necessities or decorative accessories

Easy reference—Your list of stores/catalogs:

Office supply stores	Executive Scan Card
Leather goods stores	Blue Chip Gifts & Gift Horse
J.K. Gill	Charles Keith Ltd.
	Lillian Vernon

Address book
Appointment book
Attaché case
Barometer
Book ends
Bookmark—paper, silver, leather
Bookshelves
Calculator
Calendars
Clothes brush
Clocks
Computer accessories
Lap desk
Letter opener
Organizers
Paper weight
Pens, pencils
Pocket knife
Safe for valuables
Telephone
Thermos decanter
Tools
Typewriter
Wastebasket

THE CONCEPT

EDUCATIONAL

Easy reference—Your list of stores/catalogs:

B. Dalton Bookseller	Publishers Central Bureau
Waldenbooks	Catalog (1-800-PCB-9800)
Crown Books	Sharper Image (1-800-344-4444)
Bookland	
Local bookstores	

    Books
    Chess set
    Computer games
    Course or lessons at school, museum, YMCA
    Exotic spices/herbs with notes or a book describing their origins and how they are used in recipes
    Globe
    Museum membership—historic/environmental/preservation/special interest organization

GIFTING RIGHT

EXERCISE/FITNESS
Anything that contributes to one's health and fitness, and for some, makes it easier to get started!

Easy reference—Your list of stores/catalogs:

Abercrombie & Fitch	Sharper Image
Sears Roebuck	Hammacher Schlemmer
	B.N. Genius

Bicycle
Exercise equipment—from a rowing machine to dumbbells
Health club membership
Leotard/shorts
Tennis balls
Video tape of exercise routines/aerobics

The Concept

FOOD/BEVERAGES
Consumables to be eaten immediately, or over a longer period of time

Easy reference—Your list of stores/catalogs:

Local gourmet shop/deli	Almond Plaza Catalog
Hickory Farms	(1-800-225-6887)
Cookie of the Month Club	Wolfermans Catalog
(1-800-322-6248)	(1-800-999-0169)
Fruit of the Month Club	

- Beverages, non-alcoholic a case/or 1-2 bottles if alcoholic
- Bread, freshly baked or ethnic
- Candy, dessert
- Chocolate (chocoholics will attest that they deserve their own category, separate from candy and dessert)
- Coffee, tea
- Gourmet food
- Herbs, spices
- Home-made food—pies, cookies, mustard, granola, jam, mustard, chutney, mincemeat
- Liqueur/brandy
- Special balsamic vinegar, extra virgin olive oil
- Nuts
- Wine

GADGETS
Fun or practical

Easy reference—Your list of stores/catalogs:

Abercrombie & Fitch	Enthusiasts Catalog
Hammacher Schlemmer	(603) 437-4638
Sharper Image	
B.N. Genius	
AT&T Stores	

- Answering machine with many special functions
- Desk tool or executive "toy"
- Hardware tools
- Kitchen gadget
- Sporting life equipment
- Unique telephone

REMINDER: If you want to develop any one of these ideas into a more exciting, creative, funny or luxurious gift, refer to Chapter Five, "Creative Combinations." For example, "candles" listed on the next page may appear to be too understated as a gift, until you remember that "candles" can mean one 3" multi-colored candle hand-crafted by an artist, or a whole box of plain 10" or 12" tapered dripless candles. For a more significant occasion, you could give candlesticks, with or without the candles. As with all products or ideas that you come across in this book, or as you window shop, think of these as ideas, not the only choice. You must take the ideas and shape them into a personalized gift by adding some of your own "twists" to the gift presentation.

THE CONCEPT

HOBBY/INTERESTS
What contributes to a hobby? What can you give that starts a person on a new activity, adds an accessory or replaces worn equipment for an established hobby?

Easy reference—Your list of stores/catalogs:

Brookstone	Hammacher Schlemmer
Trak Auto	The Enthusiasts Catalog
Art Supply Stores	
Toys R Us	
Local stamp/coin shops	

- Artist supplies
- Astronomy instruments
- Auto accessories
- Barbeque equipment
- Bird feeder
- Birdhouse
- Camera and accessories
- Ear phones
- Hammock
- Metronome
- Microscope
- Needlepoint kit
- Reading lamp
- Seeds

HOME FURNISHINGS/DECORATIVE

Mentally walk through every door and room of the giftee's home. What do they have on their walls, or tables? What accessories do they have? What type of items fit their personal tastes?

Easy reference—Your list of stores/catalogs:

Pier 1 Imports	Sears Catalog
Lord & Taylor	J.C. Penney Catalog
Nieman-Marcus	Montgomery Ward Catalog
Broadway	

- Bedspread hanger
- Blanket
- Candle snuffer
- Candles
- Candlesticks
- Ceiling fan
- Decorative accessory
- Decorative hardware
- Door knocker
- Doormat
- Figurines in porcelain, bronze
- Fire escape ladder
- Fireplace accessory—screen, log carrier/holder
- Flowers, silk or fresh
- Footstool
- Frames
- Furniture
- Hangers, wood
- Houseware
- Humidor
- Hurricane lamp
- Key rack/holder
- Ladder
- Lamp—desk, reading, bed, floor, piano, antique Tiffany
- Linens, bed
- Linens, table
- Mirrors
- Prints
- Rugs
- Sculpture
- Smoking accessories
- Telephone
- Towels
- Towels, guest
- Vase
- Wine rack

THE CONCEPT

HOME—OUTDOORS

Ask yourself if the gift should be practical, durable, decorative or fun?

Easy reference—Your list of stores/catalogs:

Sears	L.L. Bean Catalog
J.C. Penney	Eddie Bauer
K-Mart	
Nurseries	
Department Stores	

- Barbeque equipment
- Bird house/feeder & seeds
- Books (gardening, bird watching, etc.)
- Door knocker
- Doormat
- Hammock
- Lawn furniture
- Rakes, grass shears, pruner
- Seeds
- Shoe or boot "scraper" for front door
- Tree or bush to plant outdoors
- Weather vane

GIFTING RIGHT

KITCHENWARE

Anything that traditionally is used in a kitchen, from salad bowls to the most esoteric accessories, large or small, that contributes to the creation of any dish.

Easy reference—Your list of stores/catalogs:

Brookstone	Service Merchandise
William Sonoma Store &	
Catalog (415) 421-4242	
Best	

Chinese cookery—bamboo steamer, wok, chopsticks
Coffee maker
Cookbook
Cookware
Kitchen accessory
Kitchen gadgets
Microwave dish
Osterizer
Salad bowl

The Concept

LEISURE/OUTDOORS
What does the person do for leisure or vacations—beach, ball games, take walks, or read?

Easy reference—Your list of stores/catalogs:

L.L. Bean	Sharper Image
Eddie Bauer	

- Beach items
- Binoculars
- Books (backpacking, travel, etc.)
- Knapsack
- Picnic basket
- Sleeping bag
- Walking stick

GIFTING RIGHT

SERVING PIECES
For Entertaining—Eating/Drinking

Easy reference—Your list of stores/catalogs:

William Sonoma _____   _____

Nieman-Marcus _____   _____

Broadway _____   _____

Saks Fifth Avenue _____ _____

_____   _____

- Bar accessories—basic tools or crazy gadgets
- Barbeque equipment, utensils
- Brandy snifters
- Cappuccino maker
- Child's dinnerware set
- Cocktail napkins—with humorous sayings, name or initials
- Coffee mug
- Coffee pot for serving
- Decanter
- Dining accessories
- Dishes, bowls, cups and saucers
- Escargot utensils
- Expresso pot
- Glasses for drinking—paper plastic, crystal
- Hors d'oeuvres plates, serving dishes
- Ice bucket
- Ice cream scoop
- Knives, cheese or steak
- Napkin rings
- Nutcracker
- Pitcher
- Place card holders—from silly to silver
- Salad bowl, serving and individual
- Silver tarnish cloth
- Silverware, flatware
- Tea pot
- Tray
- Trivet
- Wine caddy
- Wine coaster

The Concept

SPORTS
Think of clothes, accessories, or equipment that complement a sport.

Easy reference—Your list of stores/catalogs:

Hermans Sports Stores	L.L. Bean
Eddie Bauer	
Best	
Abercrombie & Fitch	

    Baseball glove
    Basketball, football, etc.
    Bicycle
    Caps
    Croquet set
    Fishing/hunting equipment
    Frisbee
    Games (e.g. Ring Toss)
    Health Club Membership
    Hiking boots
    Jump rope
    Riding crop
    Ski clothes/equipment
    Sweat band
    Sweatshirt and pants
    Swimming goggles, fins
    Swimming lessons
    Tennis balls, racquet
    Tennis lessons
    Volleyball net

STOCKING STUFFERS—BIG & SMALL

Catch-all for sentimental or fun gifts that are being given strictly for personal reasons and do not fit into another category. These are the gifts given "just because." They can be totally frivolous. Or, there are traditional or sentimental reasons attached to the gift.

Easy reference—Your list of stores/catalogs:

Spencer Gifts	Harriet Carter
Hatch's	Carol Wright
J.K. Gill	Johnson-Smith
Hallmark Stores	Lillian Vernon

- Balloons
- Board game—backgammon, Monopoly
- Book
- Cards, playing
- Christmas ornaments
- Cigars
- Current fad item
- Dominoes
- Flashlight
- Goldfish bowl
- Greeting cards
- Kite
- Magnets
- Mask—animal, witch, politician or movie star, or Batman
- Miniatures—whatever the recipients cannot afford—Rolls Royce, Lear jet, model of dream home
- Mistletoe
- Mobiles
- Model, cars or airplanes
- Music box
- Perfume
- Personalized product—frame, pillow, mug, towel, with one's name or initials
- Pet accessory
- Photograph
- Plant
- Puzzle, jig-saw or for desk
- Sachéts, handmade
- Savings bond
- Sounds of nature on tape cassette—ocean, rain, etc.
- Stuffed animal
- Subscription to magazine
- T-shirt
- Your time

The Concept

TRAVEL

What would make someone's travel easier, more organized or pleasant?

Easy reference—Your list of stores/catalogs:

The Literate Traveler	Airline gift catalogs
Luggage Stores	
B. Dalton Bookseller	
Waldenbooks	
Gift/Department stores	

- Champagne
- Cosmetic bags
- Jewelry roll
- Luggage
- Passport case
- Photo album
- Portable safe
- Shoe bags
- Theater tickets at city of destination
- Toiletry case
- Travel book (on specific location)
- Travel guide and map
- Travel iron
- Travel journal/diary
- Wallet

THREE

THE EASY WAY TO PROFILE GIFT RECIPIENTS

If you have difficulty determining what gift to present, you probably could use a more effective way to describe a person—in terms of gift giving. Many people struggle with descriptions, i.e., he's funny, he's tall, he works, he has a family. These may help refine your choice, but you need a better, quicker way to pinpoint what gift would be most appropriate.

In this chapter you will learn the right questions to ask about a person for whom you must choose a gift. You will also learn that there are obvious clues available to speed your gift search. These clues will aid you in choosing the most appropriate gift for your best friend, or an obligatory gift for an acquaintance.

For any person for whom you must get a gift, you'll almost always know their general age and your relationship. In terms of gift giving, there are only **five age groups** and **three types of relationships.** An understanding of each will guide you to the most appropriate gifts and fewer *faux pas*.

The Five Age Groups For Gift Giving

When it comes to gift giving, everyone falls into one of five age groups. It is not precisely one's chronological age, but one's stage in life that immediately narrows our gift choices, or how we proceed in determining the best gift suggestions. *The five age groups in gift giving are:*

Children
Teens
Acquiring Adults
Established Adults
Seniors

The Concept

CHILDREN
This is the age group from infant to teen. Because children spend a majority of their time under adult supervision, you'll get the best gift ideas from those who spend time with the child. Therefore, if you're not up on the latest fads or trends or what currently interests a child, ask their parents, teachers, or babysitters.

You could safely get a specialty store certificate so the child can select his favorite item within a given category: ice cream shop, fast-food hamburger or pizza shop, local toy or sporting goods store. Or present a ticket to any parent-sanctioned event: a movie, sporting event, or a circus.

Barring information from these primary sources, ask friends with children the same age, or ask sales personnel at toy stores or children's gift shops. Ask more than one person to get a variety of good ideas.

NOTE: Babies are not included in a separate gift age, because baby presents are appreciated most often by the parents since "little ones" aren't old enough to respond to most gifts.

TEENAGERS
Being aware of fads is important. But it's safest to ask parents or close friends of the teen for ideas. If you get something tangible like clothes or accessories, make sure it won't make the Giftee uncomfortable; peer pressure is overwhelming at this age. A safer bet is to present a certificate to a clothes or music store, tickets to a music event (someone you know they like) or coupons for video rentals of their choice.

Intangible, successful gifts might include an "outing" to a play or a day in the country or city, local or far away.

NOTE: "Young Adults," approximately 18-25 years old, can fall into either the previous Teenagers category or Acquiring Adults. Young adults are those who have graduated from high school or college, started graduate work, or entered the workforce. They may be acquiring functional items as they begin their independent lives, like professional work clothes or household items, but they may still delight in totally frivolous youth-oriented gifts.

ADULTS-ACQUIRING
This group has been in the work force for at least a few years or many years. For the most part, they are more mature. Whether married or single, they have generally established homes and an adult lifestyle. They are beginning to acquire longer-lasting, durable items whether it is clothes, kitchen appliances or decorative household items. Their ages range roughly from 25-39.

ADULTS-ESTABLISHED
This group, generally from 40-65, does not need the basics of life (although, occasionally, replacements are needed). Unless you are aware of specific needed items, it's better to present personal or sentimental gifts such as photographs, artist commissioned drawings of current or past homes, or homemade items, such as writing poems or music for the occasion. If you have a talent for making anything—from crafts to food—now's the time to consider it as a gift.

Non-personal decorative items can easily clutter a home already filled with items collected over many years. For this reason, consumable items are most successful as gifts. Consider the lifestyle. Would a fine cognac or case of diverse beer be suitable, or tickets to a sports event or play?

SENIORS
This group does not necessarily have "everything," but they often have collected what they want or need. So, consider lifestyles and health. What's important to them? What is their work or hobby? Would an electric blanket be appropriate, some books or audio cassettes, or dinner at a favorite restaurant, or sending them on a cruise? Consider a VCR, rental of tapes or an offer to do repairs around the house? Should they receive something for the home, hobby, for comfort, convenience or merely pleasure and fun?

The Concept

Your Relationship With The Giftee

The next area that determines the most appropriate gifts is your relationship with the Giftee or recipient.

There are only three categories in terms of gift giving:
  Close friends—Includes close relatives, lovers, best friends
  Casual friends/acquaintances—includes distant relatives
  Office/work colleagues

CLOSE FRIENDS
This group includes anyone with whom you have a warm or close relationship—friends, and perhaps, but not always, relatives. Because these are persons in whom you confide and with whom you socialize, gifts can be informal, formal, sentimental or outrageous.

These are the persons in your life that get the most meaningful or thoughtful gifts. They are special, so giving them gifts that say "I love you," "I care for you," or "I think you're the greatest," will succeed every time.

NOTE: "Lovers"—The principles that apply to gifts for the "Close Friends" category also apply to gifts for lovers. The added difference is that those gifts are also more intimate, romantic or sexy.

CASUAL FRIENDS/ACQUAINTANCES
Gifts for this group tend to be more impersonal or "safe," because these are persons you do not know well. They might be future good friends, but they aren't yet. The acquaintances category includes persons to whom you give obligatory gifts. There's no need to suffer anguish trying to locate a gift with a personal statement for acquaintances; just try to be considerate—and use the ideas in this book such as the generic gift list.

OFFICE/WORK COLLEAGUES
Gifts should be more formal generally, unless the office is "like family" or the person you are giving to is a good friend as well. If you know little about a colleague's outside interests and lifestyles, stick to gifts that adapt to what the occasion

demands. (Refer to Chapter Five for examples of office/work gifts).

Specific Profile Questions

In order to provide more personalized clues and refine your choice, it will be helpful to quickly review the following questions. Don't agonize over any question. React only to questions in which answers pop out at you. (Note: you should have a specific person in mind.)

ABOUT INTERESTS

Interests/Hobbies: What does he/she do with his/her leisure time? Does he/she prefer active sports or a quieter lifestyle?

Where does he/she spend most of his/her time? At work, at home, with a hobby? (It's always a good idea to add to the comforts or enjoyment of where a person *must* spend time, as well as where they *choose* to spend time.)

Is an important event forthcoming in their life? Travel? Career move? Wedding? Birth of a baby?

Is there an activity they love, but rarely do, because of cost, time or hassle? This leads to "service" gifts such as taking someone to dinner, theater, or sports event. You can arrange for a limousine to get them there, or for a babysitter (or sit yourself), so the couple can take the night off or go away for an entire weekend. You could personalize a handmade gift certificate

LIFESTYLE TASTES THAT REFINE GIFT CHOICES

Lifestyle Tastes: Is his/her everyday style formal, fancy, relaxed, or casual? Is he/she very social, image or designer-conscious? Or is most of their entertaining done casually, or quietly, at home?

Personal preferences: What kinds of things does he/she collect or admire? Antiques, fads, high-tech products, handmade items, practical or frivolous items?

The Concept

Formal or Informal Lifestyle: Does he/she entertain with crystal and silver, gourmet food and Irish linen, or paper napkins, home style food and placemats? Everyone likes to splurge, rich or poor. Respond to his/her lifestyle. For a family economizing, you might get a pack of fancy, colorful paper napkins or a box of steaks. For an affluent family, a splurge food might be something more perishable—fresh lobster flown in that day—or for fun—an entire lamb, and have a dozen friends show up to help eat it.

Is their lifestyle cluttered or tidy? Are they collectors of magazines/newspapers and knick knacks or do they avoid clutter of any type? Everyone has a comfort level; try always to notice what your friend(s) prefer. [TIP: Generic gifts such as frames are good for either category.]

Wrap-Up

As you will discover, selecting a gift is much easier when you are able to classify the gift recipient's age group and your relationship in terms of gift giving. You still should not hesitate to ask friends, relatives and colleagues for clues.

To aid you in remembering these facts, keep the tear-out sheet (last page) with you in your wallet or purse. It lists the age groups, types of relationships and questions you need to ask when profiling the recipients.

FOUR

THE OCCASIONS

Define Occasions & Discover Ideas Automatically

If you were going to a wedding would you give a pound of cheddar cheese as a gift? What about giving your dinner party hostess a radio? It's unlikely that these ideas would cross your mind because the occasions themselves dictate other types of gifts. When you venture out to find a gift, remember that the occasion further defines what type of gift to give.

For example, once-in-a-lifetime occasions (weddings, special anniversaries) suggest gifts different than gifts for perennial occasions (birthday, holidays). Weddings imply gifts that are attractive and will last a long time—crystal, clocks, decorative gifts. Annual gifts can be less durable—food and drink, clothes, theater tickets—or strictly functional—appliances, computer software.

ANNUAL HOLIDAYS, BIRTHDAYS

For annual occasions such as birthdays and holidays, it is appropriate to give almost anything needed, wanted or unexpected. Since these are not one-time-only gifts, they don't have to last for 40 years.

There is more flexibility with which to present things that are:

Practical	Kitchen appliances/nightgowns;
Emotional	Silly novelties (a new game or the latest fad); or
Durable	Major gifts or extraordinary mementoes; (jewelry, musical instruments, furniture, artwork).

The Concept

If you want gifts to last throughout the year, consider magazine subscriptions; having flowers delivered monthly; providing a personal service of something you do well (a series of guitar, sewing or dancing lessons, and even household repairs and chores); or, perhaps, movie tickets for every other month.

Although you may still come up with a uniquely personal gift, the pressure is off for getting a once-in-a-lifetime gift, such as those given at weddings.

Hanukkah holds a different tradition than other annual holidays. For each of the eight nights of Hanukkah a candle is lit and a small gift is presented. (Sometimes families may choose to give one or two big presents instead). If you're partaking in this Jewish holiday for the first time, ask your Jewish friends if their family has special traditions.

ANNIVERSARIES

Mandatory observance of wedding anniversaries is usually left to immediate families. Gifts or parties for anniversaries are at the discretion of friends, family and close colleagues to arrange.

If an anniversary date, other than for a wedding, is important to someone, he or she no doubt would appreciate remembrance of it by friends or relatives. In some instances a card may be sufficient—or an elaborate event may be in order. It's the giver's choice. It depends upon the closeness of the relationship.

WEDDINGS

A wedding gift is usually long-lasting, "beautiful," and often for the home—practical or decorative. It is best to find something that *both* the bride and groom will appreciate and use.

For younger couples marrying, practical household gifts would be most appreciated, and there are many items that are both useful and beautiful. These may in fact be luxuries the couple could not yet afford. It's an appropriate time to contribute to china, silver or crystal selections, or add to table or bed linens, blankets and plush bath towel ensembles.

Find out from relatives if the bride has registered her choices and at what store, this way you'll be sure to get what is needed and wanted. If you feel getting the registered gift isn't creative or special enough, add a little personal gift. Read Chapter Five, "The Enhancers," to learn how.

Strictly functional gifts are okay if the couple needs basic items—such as appliances, but often these are reserved for shower gifts. An expensive appliance, however, like a TV, stereo, Cuisinart or microwave, would be an appreciated wedding gift for any age. You might consider getting friends or siblings to jointly chip in for more expensive gifts.

SECOND WEDDINGS

These are not unlike first wedding gifts. However it is likely that the couple has already acquired the basics for setting up a home. Your gifts should be suited to "Established Adults" (see Chapter Three). Between the two of them, they may have two toaster ovens and no coffee pot. So, if you are unsure of their appliance needs, generic gifts, like an interesting picture frame, should be considered (Chapter Eight).

Functional gifts that are the best of any line, could, perhaps, replace older, well-worn items they already have. In fact, focus on items that are decorative and functional like candlesticks or serving pieces—beyond basic knives and forks and plates. Or try a functional "service" gift for a couple with young children, by presenting a bottle of champagne with a note offering to babysit while they're on their honeymoon.

Expensive splurge items (a sleek leather telephone or one with Mickey Mouse), or an expensive appliance like a VCR, Cuisinart, would also be successful, or any new state-of-the-art gadget.

WEDDING SHOWERS

Often a theme is stated—kitchen, lingerie, bath and bedroom—which makes giving easier. When there are no guidelines, you can get something practical or not, but it's always nice for the bride to get personal splurge gifts because the shower is a celebration for her. Therefore, lingerie is always welcome. Brainstorm with other friends of the bride or

The Concept

relatives for possible suggestions. Even if you do not get specifics, you will surely get clues!

If a "co-ed" shower is more appropriate—or requested by the couple—consider a wine, bar or garden shower. Entertaining presents can include special bottles of wine, glasses, cork screws, bar utensils and other items. Garden items can include tools, plants (for indoor and out), sun hats, knee pads, and even patio furniture.

BABY SHOWERS

One young mother told me that pretty little dresses are lovely to look at, but infants live in warm, soft terry cloth and cotton knit outfits which must be changed and washed frequently. They aren't as beautiful or as much fun to present as dresses or little boy suits, but the mother will appreciate them. If you must get dress-up clothes get them in larger sizes when the child will actually be wearing them.

For first-time mothers, buy practical gifts for the baby that will make the early months more convenient for the mother. In order for you to add pizazz to these functional gifts, combine it with a "contrasting" gift that balances your selection. See Chapter Five, "The Enhancers" for more ideas.

For example:
>a white cardigan sweater (*fashionable*, yet *useful* and warm) could be presented with
>
>a rattle (*functional* and *fun*), or a stuffed animal (a cuddly toy—not "needed" but destined for love—from the *emotional* gift function).
>
>Or a *durable* gift (a Savings Bond or an engraved silver cup) can be given with a *silly* gift (pacifiers for mom, dad and baby).

For mothers who already have children, think of a small present for baby and something nice for the mother, like bubble bath, a new bathrobe or a portable radio/cassette with earphones for late night feedings.

GIFTING RIGHT

HOST/HOSTESS
These are really token gifts of appreciation so you needn't get an expensive, serious or durable gift. Get something that can be used in the home, such as a nice food treat (homemade cookies or a jar of gourmet jam) or a bottle of wine or champagne. Also consider fun items like cocktail napkins with humorous sayings or arrange to imprint napkins with the person's name, initials or nickname. A plant or flowers also are excellent choices.

NEW HOME, HOUSE WARMING
These gifts should relate in some way to the home—a barbeque grill or accessories, a door knocker, a decorative china bowl or kitchen appliances—or to the comfort and pleasure of the entire family.

Do you want something that will add to the investment of the house? How about bushes, flowers or a tree to plant outdoors? Or is it more appropriate to get something to ease their arrival into the new neighborhood? How about a detailed map of the new location? Include a list of the most practical stores—from hardware to food sources. Or present homemade food, wine, beer, a case of soda, freshly-cut flowers or a potted plant.

Include a personal message that welcomes your friend(s) into the new neighborhood or city and wishes them well in their new location.

GET WELL
Since the aim of a "get well" gift is to make someone smile, help the person in their recuperation or remind them you are thinking of them. Humorous or warm conceptual presents will be appropriate. A silly card or personal mushy note may be absolutely perfect!

If you want to give a pleasant visual, send flowers, a plant, stuffed animal, poster or large card. If the patient might enjoy or need an activity to do in bed or if house-bound, consider a humor book, board or card games, yarn for knitting, or movie rentals for the VCR. Or present something they can look forward to using when they are well.

The Concept

JUST BECAUSE
"Just because" gifts can take any form. These are the unexpected presents. They are tokens of friendship, appreciation or romance. Flowers, candy, a book, or a bottle of wine can be given just because "I love you," to "thank you," to say "I'm sorry"—just because, for any reason.

Spontaneous gifts fall into this category. When you buy something because it reminds you of someone, and you just can't wait until their birthday to give it to them, give it to them "just because."

OFFICE OCCASIONS
Gifts for the office can be for retirements, for birthdays, or for holiday gifts. You may also consider giving gifts for someone getting a promotion, doing a great job on a special project, as congratulations for getting a contract, or as a token upon return from a trip or vacation in another faraway city or overseas. Chapter Five, "The Enhancers," includes a section on dozens of office gift ideas, but Chapter Twelve includes "1001 gift ideas" based on your relationship with the person and whether you want a decorative, functional, durable or emotional gift.

Birthday
When gifts are given for a birthday at the office, it usually means the office has a friendly atmosphere like a family, so the gift selection can follow the rules for friends or family, because gifts need not be so formal.

Holidays
If you work in an office where gifts are obligatory during Holidays, get ideas from the generic gift list (Chapter Eight), where you can find many appropriate items that come in a variety of styles or prices and are as formal or informal as you wish, depending on your add-ons and the way you package them.

For both friendly or less-chummy offices, it is always nice to give something you think the person would want or use. Does your assistant or secretary wear an accessory often, like earrings, a scarf or belt? If a colleague collects things on his desk, shelves or walls, get another item or something to organize or display those collections. If the person has an outside interest or hobby known to the office, contribute to that idea, individually or, perhaps, have your colleagues chip in to get one needed item.

Corporate gifts or those given to outside clients have an entirely different aura. They are more formal or impersonal (i.e., professional). There are companies that specialize in these gifts. The most common office gifts are paperweights, umbrellas, totes, calendars or appointment books.

For more creative, personalized corporate gifts, think about items that relate to and complement the company image and purpose. For the most unique gift, consider an original work of art. Consult with artists—fine artists or writers. You may get a poem etched on a plaque, or a poster, lithograph or sculpture showing the company's founder, product, mascot, building or something less formal that still visualizes what is important to the company—history, literature, art, culture.

Retirements/Leaving an organization
Usually a joint gift is presented from the entire office staff when someone leaves the company to retire, or when moving on to another job. The generic gift list has many useful ideas. A person retiring may be planning to travel, stay home and entertain more, or work on a hobby. Brainstorm with colleagues about gifts that relate to those interests and determine what the person wants—something for the home, their hobby or for a new office. Don't get a clock, for example, no matter how nice, if the person is retiring and doesn't have much planned. The clock might be symbolic of ticking away the hours and minutes of one's life, which would be depressing and not a positive send-off.

Tokens upon return from vacations/trips
These gifts need not be expensive, and, in fact, should not be because they are tokens of appreciation or friendship, not meant to obligate the recipients into returning the favor. You are not even obliged by protocol to get something for friends or staff members if you travel; it depends on your style and common sense. For types of items to present, look for

The Concept

something that is indicative of the city/country you have visited. It can be practical or decorative.

The size of the gift(s) depends on how many gifts you want to take home or will fit into your luggage—the latter being the reason why token gifts from trips are traditionally small.

THE ENHANCERS
FIVE

Ideas That Enhance Any Gift

Occasionally, you will locate the *almost* perfect gift. Almost perfect, because you feel that it needs "something more." It just doesn't seem complete.

For example, you are planning to get your closest friend at work a gift and have budgeted about $15. But before you find that gift, you discover a coffee mug with a whimsical saying that is perfect for your friend. As wonderfully funny as the mug is, you don't think a $5 mug is substantial enough by itself for such a close friend. You feel you need to get something else. But what?

That's where enhancing a gift can help.

Any item can be made to seem more substantial by adding contrasts or enriching its texture in a number of ways. Sometimes you add to the wrapping. But as you will learn, you can add to the inside of the package too.

ENHANCER #1:   **Add Visual Texture & Color Contrasts**

Professional cooks know that good-tasting food is not enough. The meal must be visually attractive; each dish balanced in color and texture. Apply that principle to your gifts.

The White Towels Example

Decorate the Outside

A few sets of white terry cloth bath towels are a fine wedding gift, if you've determined they are needed by the couple, but in white they can easily appear plain (i.e., not substantial enough) in a white box with white tissue paper. If a gift appears plain—even though it's a great gift—*add some color to it.* At a minimum, use snappy wrapping paper and ribbons. Make them look more substantial by wrapping them in contrasting (green, purple) tissue paper or spruce up the

THE ENHANCERS

wrapping with an extra large colorful ribbon. A big plaid or flowered ribbon, for example, would make any gift more festive, even a plain green plant.

You don't need to spend a lot. If your budget is very tight, find a remnant of fabric or dried flowers or anything that would "contrast" the gift and perk it up.

Decorate the Inside

In addition to wrapping the outside, place a few small items of contrasting color *inside* the box to add visual appeal. Colorful decorative soaps or sachets could be added to the towels. What about monogramming the towels? Or, if your budget allows present the towels **in** something, like a new wicker hamper.

ENHANCER #2: **For More Texture, Add The Unexpected**

Adding "color" can also mean adding pizazz. Add other types of texture. Add the unexpected.

> Tie balloons to the ribbon.
>
> Add an Art Deco pin, one silk flower or 10 Tootsie Roll pops.
>
> Give a pair of chopsticks with a calendar featuring oriental art.
>
> How about a separately wrapped gift of candles given with a book that was originally written before electricity was discovered.

In other words, add any "extra" you like to the gift. Stocking stuffers are fun and they give pleasure in May, July or September!

Creative Gift Combinations

Let's say a successful male executive receives a combination gift of a photo of his pet dog, a pack of baseball cards and a box of penny candies. The items are not related but they all point to the child within the man, bringing back fond memories. You can be sure he will appreciate the thoughtfulness of the gift.

As you will learn, a more appealing "presentation" can be created by combining two or more gift items. Like above, however, it should not happen haphazardly. And like the visual presentations described previously, you need to create a thoughtful balance.

ENHANCER #3: **Add A Contrasting Gift**

Add contrast to the "base" or main gift. Determine its characteristics and contrast it with the opposite. Enclose a small gift with a large gift. Give a humorous or silly gift with a practical gift. Or an expensive gift with an inexpensive sentimental gift.

Examples:
    Functional (kitchen towels) with silly/fun (cookie cutters)
    Expensive (tea pot) with inexpensive (tea bags)
    Formal (crystal candy dish) with sentimental (Hershey's chocolate kisses)
    Educational (cookbook) with splurge food (smoked oysters)

ENHANCER #4: **Contrast Gift Purposes**

As Chapter One states, every gift has a message or "purpose." If your gift needs "something," you may also wish to include an item with another purpose.

For example, if you give your sister a cutting board and knife which is strictly *practical*, you might get a small personal gift that would satisfy the *emotional* category such as a sentimental Christmas ornament, a favorite food or candy, something hand-made by you, or a piece of clothing or jewelry, if you can spend more.

Or, if you want to contrast the practical cutting board with something *decorative*, you might give flowers, a picture or photograph, or clothing accessories. Also, since the cutting board is durable, you might contrast it with something *non-durable* like flowers or food.

The Enhancers

ENHANCER #5: **Theme Gifts**

Multiple Unrelated Gifts

There is no rule that says you must buy *one* gift only. If the gift you want to give is not substantial enough, or you haven't come across that one perfect gift in your price range (what you want to or think you should spend), present two or more gifts. They can be presented at one time or spread out over the course of a party or an entire day. *Multiple unrelated gifts* can be presented as a combined package through the use of themes.

How To Create Themes

You can create the theme before or after locating a gift. For either method, you must begin by knowing something about the person's lifestyle and interests. Use the quick way to profile a person in Chapter Three.

For example, if you know someone wants a thermos coffee cup for use while commuting by car to the office, locate three gifts—one each for the car, the office and home.

If the person is a self-improver, present a package of gifts for the body, the mind, and the spirit. If someone is a homebody, present gifts for the living room (book), bathroom (bubble bath), and kitchen (food).

More Examples of Gifts & Themes

Five sample theme combinations follow, with suggested gifts for each category:

#1 Gifts for the mind, body and spirit:

Mind	**Body**	**Spirit**
Calculator	Suntan oil	Tape of great music
Book*	Exercise equipment	Two theater tickets

*Never overlook books. There are books for most categories and themes, lifestyles and interests, from serious to silly.

Gifting Right

#2 Gifts for a rainy day and a sunny day:

Rainy Day	**Sunny Day**
Concert tickets	Tickets to a frisbee or volleyball match on a beach
Jigsaw puzzle	Portable backgammon
Potted flowers	Seeds for garden

#3 Gifts for laughter, quiet time and for parties:

For Laughter	**For Quiet Time**	**For Parties**
Book of humor	Bubble bath soap	"Win, Lose, or Draw" game
"Dirty" joke gift	Bottle of sherry	Glasses
101 balloons	A down comforter	Cheese knife

#4 Gifts for the bedroom, bathroom and den:

For bedroom	**For Bathroom**	**For den**
Sachets	Glass jar to hold cotton balls	Notepads
Mirrored Wastebasket	Wicker Wastebasket	Leather or brass Wastebasket

---

#5 Gifts for hands, eyes and ears:

Hands	**Eyes**	**Ears**
Ring	Sunglasses	Earmuffs
Thimble	Mascara	Earrings
Feather duster	TV set	Ear plugs

The Enhancers

#6 Gift goods for breakfast, lunch and dinner:

Breakfast	**Lunch**	**Dinner**
Home-made or gourmet jam	Home-made bread	Bottle of wine
Box of oranges from Florida	Fancy mustards	Box of steaks

#7 Gifts for mother, father and baby:

Mother	**Father**	**Baby**
Bubble baths	Ear plugs	Teddy bear
Tee shirt - "I'm the Mommy"	Tee shirt - "I'm the Daddy"	Tee shirt - "I'm the Baby"
Diaper bag	Back baby carrier	Hat/booties

#8 You can also present multiple gifts under one theme. Here are a number of gifts that all relate to entertainment in some way:

Entertainment theme
- Theater tickets to a smash show
- Coupons or gift certificate to local movie theater
- Opera glasses
- Tiny flashlight to read programs in dark theaters
- Jar of Orville Redenbacher's gourmet popcorn
- Blank video cassette tapes
- Certificate to rent a movie at local video shop
- Notecards with a musical logo or picture
- Books on music, art or a biography of a favorite movie star

Other themes could be:
- For night (VCR rental) and day (frisbee).
- For head (hair dryer) to toes (pedicure set).
- For work (pen) and play (tennis balls).

The possibilities are as endless as the personalities and lifestyles of those you are presenting with gifts. Brainstorm with a friend to come up with more theme and gift ideas. You are only limited by your imagination.

ENHANCER #6: **Add-ons**

Directly Related Gifts

Another way to create a combination to enhance your complete gift package is begin with a basic idea or "base" gift, and add *directly-related* items to it.

You can spend 50 cents or hundreds of dollars on add-ons. By determining the types of add-ons before you venture out, you will be guided to stores or departments with related gifts. Then, while looking in that section or shelf, you will more easily come across a marvelous item you had not previously thought of that adds balance and pizazz to your base gift.

It might be as simple as inserting something in a gift frame. Think of the great changes that could be made in your presentation by simply adding a photograph, a cartoon, a magazine illustration or a hand-written note.

How To Expand 22 Office-Related Products To Hundreds of Gift Ideas

As mentioned earlier, the personal lifestyle and home habits of office colleagues are not well known. Therefore, many office gifts must be related to the office environment. What follows are a variety of suggested office-related gifts including "add-ons" which will help you make any gift more personalized:

The Enhancers

> Key to Approximate Costs
>
> ¢ $10
> $ $25
> $$ $100
> $$$ .... over $200

Address Book

¢-$

In the office, names, addresses and telephone numbers are often organized on a Rolodex. A handsome Rolodex to match desk or surroundings would be appropriate. Or consider giving a small leather address book to use when travelling, if the executive has a Rolodex.

Add-ons

Engrave initials on the address book cover. Provide extra Rolodex cards or address book inserts. A fine pen, or pen/pencil set.

Attaché case/tote

$-$$$

This is a personal item, that should not be purchased for another unless their preference for a specific carrying case has been indicated. Since a briefcase is used daily, do not force someone to use one, if it does not represent their style or taste.

A tote, on the other hand, is not expected to be used daily (although it could). It could be used whenever it matched the colors or style of dress. Never get a canvas or vinyl tote for a person who prefers real leather, unless it's for fun (not for office). Take a look at their shoes. If they wear expensive shoes, the odds are high that they would prefer to spend more on a high quality attaché case or tote that would last years, rather then an item that was less expensive and would wear out in one or two years.

Add-ons
>Any desk accessory that might be transported in the briefcase for possible home use—a calculator, a small address book, engraved notepads, appointment book, portable dictaphone.

Barometer
>$$

For the person who has everything, or someone who likes gadgets. For a table or wall.

Add-ons
>Some barometers come with other measuring tools attached, i.e., a thermometer and hygrometer (to measure humidity).

Bookends
>¢-$$

Bookends can be humorous or elegant. For the executive, go to a leather goods/desk accessory shop, department store or even an antique shop. You'll find them in leather, brass, silver, and other materials. Bookends can be used on a shelf or on the desk.

Add-ons
>One book, two or more. If you are giving a gift to a superior, you had best not give a book on management techniques, unless it was suggested by the Giftee. Reference books are a safer bet. Or a best-selling book of fiction would be nice for home or to bring on the next business trip or vacation.

Bookmarks
>¢-$

A small thoughtful gift. Most bookmarks come in paper or leather, although some jewelry/gift stores carry them in silver, pewter or brass. You might also locate them in antique shops.

Add-ons
>Books, of course.

THE ENHANCERS

Bookshelves
$-$$$
> For bookshelves or another piece of furniture, it would be more appropriate received from family members or perhaps as a joint gift from the office staff.

Add-ons
> Books, bookends, picture frames.

Calculator
¢-$
> Calculators should bring to mind all the types of small electronic (or solar-powered) gifts you can present.

Add-ons
> Small desk items, such as notepads for brief notes or scratching out mathematical totals from the calculator.

Calendars
¢-$
> From paper versions to perennial calendars encased in attractive metal or wood frames.

Add-ons
> Anything that has to do with time management. Large monthly calendars with art works or humorous photos, or appointment organizers for the office/desk or small leather appointment books. Or present a Filofax or other notebook organizer. These organizers usually have sections for address, appointments, expenses and places to insert your calculator and checkbook.

Clothes brush
¢-$
> For the person who cares about his appearance. You know it by the way his clothes are pressed and shoes are shined. For the up and coming executive.

Add-ons
> Travel toiletry case.

Gifting Right

Coffee mug
¢-$

Mugs with funny illustrations or sayings are great as humorous gifts, or a beautiful china mug or demitasse cup/saucer for presenting a more serious image.

Add-ons

A set of four or six mugs or cups/saucers for use by office visitors.
A thermos decanter
A drip coffee pot.

Computer accessories
¢-$$$

Like most items, these can be the base gift or the add-ons.

Add-ons

Learn what the person wants or needs—software programs, blank disks, typewriter ribbon and other accessories.

Clocks
¢-$$$

From a small travel alarm clock, wall clock or table clock to a priceless grandfather clock.

Add-ons

Travel accessories
Barometer/thermometer

Frames
¢-$$

Leather frame, or hand-carved or designed wood, metal, or stone.

Add-ons

A nostalgic photograph or cartoon to insert.

Hangers, wood
¢-$

Having fine wood hangers, not metal hangers, creates

both an impressive and professional image for those in any business or profession who must entertain or meet clients or guests in their office. Joan Crawford would be pleased.

Add-ons
Cedar blocks for the closet
A box or container for gloves, scarves

Letter opener

¢-$

All types of materials and price ranges, at department stores, gift and antique shops.

Add-ons
A box of stationery
Notepads
Pens, pencils
A roll of stamps

Paper weight

¢-$$

Keep it classy, unless you're presenting it as a humorous gift.

Add-ons
Note paper to be held underneath

Pens, pencils

¢-$$$

Fine pens, pen and pencil sets, or, on a lighter side, a box of everyday felt-tip or ballpoint pens used in the office

In large cities, look in *The Yellow Pages* for stores that specialize in pens. Otherwise, you'll find them in department stores, gift shops, office supply shops, large drugstores or catalog stores (W. Bell & Company or Best), that carry desk accessories.

Add-ons
Add items that have to do with writing—a letter opener or engraved writing paper. Concentrate on practical

office items—paper stock or office organizers. If you get an expensive pen, you don't need an add-on.

Safe for valuables

$-$$$

Either a cabinet or wall safe, or a money belt for travelling.

Add-ons
$1 bill to christen the safe
Travel accessories

Stationery

¢-$$

Plain notes, with or without the person's name or initials, or paper of a good quality, heavy bond with envelopes to match, with or without engraving.

Add-ons
Pens/pencils, commemorative stamps

Thermos decanter

¢-$$

For coffee, water, and other hot or cold beverages. For the office, you can get good-looking plastic ones in solid colors, including white and black, or more formal and expensive thermos decanters in metal, suitable for any executive's office.

For more informal use, a thermos can be given for commuting, or for outdoor use on weekends. These can be found in fine department stores, or large drug, grocery or hardware stores.

Add-ons
Liquid for the thermos
Cups or glasses
Tray to carry thermos/glasses

Tools

¢-$

It never hurts for an executive to have scissors around the office, or a can or bottle opener. What about a nail clipper/file? Buy them separately or present one of the variety of Swiss Army knives. Why? They contain scissors, can or bottle openers, toothpicks, nail files, not just screwdrivers and other tools. These are easy to fit into a briefcase too and can be vital when away from the office or travelling.

Add-ons
More office tools/desk accessories

Wastebasket

¢-$$

Surprise you? Yes, it seems frivolous, until you try pricing them. The most inexpensive "executive" office wastebasket I've seen lately is one with a picture of flying geese for about $25, or in brass or leather for $100 or more. Check antique stores and flea markets where you might spot a unique wastebasket, or container to use as one. It is a very practical gift and would be a good surprise.

Add-ons
Present something in it. Small practical office supplies (paper clips, pens, pencils, telephone message pads), a ream of paper, or perhaps two gallons of popcorn, or a selection of fruit, candies or herbal teas.

Key to Approximate Costs
¢ $10
$ $25
$$ $100
$$$ .... over $200

GIFTING RIGHT

ENHANCER #7: **Present Everyday Items in Quantity**

Some items can never be substantial or exciting enough gift items by themselves. But by presenting multiple quantities, the item takes on a different quality as a gift.

For example, one bottle of mineral water or soda is not considered a gift by itself, but a case of 12 bottles would be. A case of good everyday wine would be appreciated for a family on a budget. You don't need to give the finest vintage as a gift unless the recipient's knowledge warrants the difference <u>and</u> you can afford it! Ask those who know at the wine store for a good quality wine in your price range.

What about a case of tuna fish as a house-warming gift for a large family with many lunch boxes to fill? It would be appreciated and it would also make them laugh! A box of steaks would also be an appreciated splurge.

Other foods in quantity for frequent entertainers could be an entire wheel of brie or cheddar cheese or 4-5 pounds of smoked salmon, or a 1, 2 or 5 pound container of almonds or pecans. Also check *The Yellow Pages* or ask local grocers to locate "institutional" suppliers who supply food and equipment to restaurants so you can give large quantities of cheese, meats or nuts. These organizations also have gallon containers or equally large jugs of mayonnaise and ketchup, which are not practical, but they'd be unique gifts for a person that consumed a lot of the item. (After the event's laughter is over, the gallon jugs could be donated to a local institution with many mouths to feed, if the Giftee really won't consume gallon quantities).

Although foods are a natural item to present in quantity, don't forget other items, particularly small items or services people rarely purchase or splurge on for themselves. For example, present a gift certificate for two manicures or give a coupon book for 2, 3 or 4 car washes. Or give a box of candles or fire logs.

The Enhancers

Examples of Combination Gifts

Books—You can spend $20 on one hardback book, or it would be fun for the Giftee to receive a set of six paperbacks.

There are books for every subject, from the most scholarly to the silliest.

To cheer up a friend, select books from the "humor" section. There are dozens of narrative joke books, from how to speak Southern to growing up Catholic or Jewish. Also, cartoon series books about Snoopy, Garfield or from "The Far Side" are good gifts because we are less likely to purchase them for ourselves.

Cookbooks are always appreciated by those who love to cook and entertain.

What about reference books for someone starting out in business or college? A good dictionary, thesaurus or atlas?

Don't overlook good road map books for someone with a new car or having just moved to a new city. A good city road map in a durable book format can cost $5-$10, so it's a helpful and thoughtful gift. If you want to give more, present it with a book on restaurants, or shopping and cultural activities in the new city. Or give a subscription to the city magazine or locally-oriented publication, if there is one for that particular city or region.

Containers—To present a collection of smaller items, put them in one container that can be used after the gifts are removed: a china bowl, crystal vase, brass wastebasket, or straw basket for plants or a picnic. Containers can be both functional and decorative.

If the container is the main gift or the most expensive item, you can fill it with fresh or dried flowers, crushed colored tissue paper or freshly popped popcorn. Be creative! Ask yourself what other small items—either functional, edible or decorative—might enhance the container and the presentation?

If the items are being presented just for fun, the container need not be expensive or fancy. The little gifts can be put in a big box that, wrapped, looks like a serious gift until it's opened. Or if you want an equally clever container to match the gag gifts, look in unexpected places for containers—hardware stores (aluminum water pails, colorful mini-trash cans), office supply stores (in/out boxes), bath or closet accessory shops (shoe or laundry bags, tissue box covers, soap dishes or wicker hampers), flea markets (straw baskets, brass bowls) or your attic (antique trunk, Uncle Frank's top hat).

Desk Accessories—There are many practical gifts in this category for the executive, student or for home use—to write letters, organize budgets or make grocery lists. These include note pads, frames, letter openers, stationery, pen and pencil sets, wastebaskets (leather or brass).

Visit a stationery shop or section of a department store, an office supply store, or a fine leather goods or gift shop that carries office accessories. You'll get plenty of ideas. Ask the sales personnel for ideas in your budget range. Other sections in this book discuss desk accessories and related ideas, including the section on frames that follows.

Food—Wandering around the gourmet section of a food shop will give you ideas. But don't overlook non-gourmet items. They, too, can be expensive and a splurge. If you know of food or condiments someone loves but rarely purchases, add them to the package.

Combine the items thoughtfully. Are they to be *eaten immediately or over a longer period?* Are the items meant to be eaten *during cocktail time* (pate, cheeses, gherkin pickles, and crackers); *for a picnic* (French bread, cheeses, salamis, fancy mustards, fresh pears, a bottle of wine, and cookies), or would you prefer all the items be *fruits* or *sweets* (an assortment of chocolates, fudge sauce for ice cream, candied jellies); or all *condiments* (mustards, chutneys and relishes, mincemeat or jellies).

Remember, the key is to personalize the gift. A can of mandarin oranges, a box of Oreo cookies, or candies the Giftee ate as a child, are just as effective, and may be more so, than caviar and goose liver paté. Think about who you are giving the gift to and for what purpose. To impress? Or to tickle a person and make him or her smile?

Frames—If the frame is meant for the office, you can combine it with desk accessories, such as a letter opener, a note pad or pen, or state-of-the-art office gadgets.

To personalize a gift of a frame for close friends and relatives, add a photograph of yourself. If you are not comfortable giving a photo of yourself, locate a photo or picture of someone or something the person would treasure. A framed picture of their spouse or children would be an excellent gift for the home or the office. Another is a picture of the house they grew up in.

If the frame is sufficient without a photo, but you do not want to present an empty frame, put a humorous picture or cartoon in it or something clearly not meant to be in the frame ultimately. It might be a handwritten note from you, or the logo of a company with which the person has an association, a photo of a TV or movie star, or a stock exchange listing from a newspaper, circling stock the person owns—hopefully going up. You can even put patterned wrapping paper inside the frame to add to the visual treat of opening the gift box.

If the frame is clearly outstanding on its own, it is not necessary to enhance it with more than simple but elegant wrapping paper and ribbon. If you are framing a sentimental or equally impressive personal photograph with a gorgeous frame, that's double whammy! You don't need to overdo the wrapping or extras in that case.

Serving Pieces—For a gift of wine glasses, add a bottle of wine or a case of wine. Likewise, brandy, liqueur or ice tea glasses can be presented with the associated liquid or tea bags.

If an Expresso pot is the main gift, add a pound of fresh-ground Expresso coffee, coffee bean grinder, demitasse cups and spoons, or gourmet cheeses, dried fruits, cakes or candies to serve with the Expresso. A wide range of unique serving pieces can be found at flea markets for a few dollars or for ten times that at department or antique stores. Cheese or canape knives or cake servers are functional and they rarely need to identically match the design of other serving pieces, so individual pieces can be given.

Summary

You can now see that any item can be enhanced by the way you package it—by adding other items to balance the base item, using themes to create combination gift packages or by adding products or visuals to the outside wrapping. You now know the basic formulas for creating your own successful gift packages. You have learned how and why packaging the inside gift is as important as the outside gift wrapping to create a visual treat for the Giftee. If you are not comfortable creating your ideas from scratch, use store and advertising displays for ideas—and *Gifting Right,* of course.

THE ORGANIZERS

SIX

KEEPING TRACK THE EASY WAY

As you begin to incorporate the *Gifting Right* way of thinking into your life, you will want to keep track of great gift ideas, and anticipate birthdays and anniversaries. There are a few methods that will not burden your busy life.

Remembering Gift Ideas

In order to make "gift time" less frustrating, you need a method for remembering gift ideas when you need them.

The quickest—although not the best method—of remembering great gift ideas from catalogs or advertisements, is to toss them into a drawer.

This method will get you decent results, but there's a better way to compile personalized gift clues with very little effort.

TRACKING IDEA #1:   Write Down Clues As Soon As You Recognize Them!

As you work, laugh, or live with potential giftees, it will become obvious what activities or events are important to these special people in your life.

Observe friends' and colleagues' interests. This can mean hobbies, or specific product needs as well as strong preferences for color or styles. Keep alert to anything that they indicate, directly and indirectly, they need or would like. **Then, write it down as soon as possible—on a cocktail napkin, movie ticket stub or any scrap of paper handy, to stuff in your pocket, if necessary.** If you carry an address book with you, write (in pencil, so you don't permanently mess up your book) gift ideas and friends' interests in your book after their names.

Don't wait until their birthday (or other event) to try to recall that terrific gift idea. In fact, don't even wait until you get home! By having the foresight to jot it down, you will save yourself from racking your brain later on with "What shall I get? What shall I get!!?!!!"

In addition to observing friends' interests in activities, **pay attention to clues that occur during less obvious situations.** For example, if you are at a friend's house and while serving wine, a glass breaks and your friend mentions he or she has broken a number of glasses and has few nice wine glasses left, make a note of it. If a friend dotes on a pet or spends hours caring for plants, make a note that these things are important.

Color and style, not just products, play an important role. What color is a friend's living room, bedroom, or china pattern? These colors have usually been selected with considerable thought and because of a strong preference. Are the fabrics busy or stark? These also are clues to a person's taste.

Take stock of your friends interests. Mentally walk through a day with them. You don't necessarily have to come up with specific gift ideas at first, but by noting friends' interests, hobbies, desires or needs, throughout the year, *you will cut gift selection anxiety in half.* Once you know some of the person's interests, habits and current lifestyle, your choices will fall into obvious categories. Are they workaholics? Are they sports jocks? Or, are they couch potatoes? What are their hobbies? Do they like magic tricks? Do they spend every free weekend sailing or visiting antique shops? Or are they homebodies?

Jot down any answers; don't try to get perfect answers. I'm sure you'd agree that it's better to have five ideas for birthday and holiday gifts than none. You can then choose from the best of them, depending on your relationship with the person and your budget at the time a gift is needed. Even if your budget is limited, by noting these gift clues, you may find appropriate items on sale during the year. And, as the gift

The Organizers

event draws near, you can further personalize the gift or make it extra special by enhancing it with the ideas found in Chapter Five.

TRACKING IDEA #2: Incorporate Gift Ideas Into Present Recordkeeping System

With simple bookkeeping, you can present successful gifts every time. Rather than making new records at first, make it as easy as possible. Incorporate gift ideas into your present record keeping systems. For example, most people have a system for recording names and addresses at home or in the office. Next time you learn about someone's interests or hobbies, needs or "wish" items, write them next to their name in your address book or Rolodex file. Also, note significant dates by each name. (A simple system for remembering dates is described below). Write ideas in pencil, if you wish, which will give you the option of transferring your notes to a separate place later on and allow you to erase your notes and keep your address book from getting too cluttered or messy.

TRACKING IDEA #3: For More Elaborate Recordkeeping— An Easier Way

If you want to keep track of a person's interests and hobbies in a separate place, the following information could be written on index cards, one for each person. *Remember, too, that over the years, interests and lifestyles may change, but not drastically, so you shouldn't need to redo the cards from scratch each year.* For the occasional projects that are of a temporary nature or special events occurring once only, mark the card in pencil.

GIFTING RIGHT

Card Front:

NAME

Birthdate

Other Dates

Significant Others

Specific Gift Ideas

Gift(s) Given Last Year

Explanation of Categories

Name & Birthdate. Type or write in ink; dates don't change.

Other dates. Anniversary dates. There are other anniversary dates besides wedding dates. One can celebrate the anniversary of a significant event, either personal or job-related. What has been important to the person? Has an event changed his/her life?

Significant Others' names & birthdates. It may help you to know names and some dates of those close to the person. Don't spend extra time trying to get these dates. Add this information as you learn it during the normal course of spending time with your friends and family. Obviously, the better you know someone the more details you will have about special people in their lives.

Suggested specific gift ideas. (Put in pencil because these will be modified and changed annually).

Gift given last year. This is so as not to embarrass by giving a repeat gift, which otherwise can easily happen when you're buying for a lot of people.

The Organizers

Card Back:

Interests/Hobbies
Lifestyle/Work Habits
Sizes
Color Preferences
Other

Explanation of Card Back Categories

Interests/Hobbies: Do they have a hobby like stamp collecting, magic, computers, tennis, reading or photography? Or do they prefer to socialize, entertain or go to parties? Many people have more than one interest, so hopefully, you have been able to determine at least one. If they seem to have a million interests, get them something to help organize their thoughts or life...a book, like this one...or consumables that won't add clutter to their life.

Lifestyle/Work Habits: Do they prefer leisure time or work? Is their lifestyle formal or informal? Do they spend more time at home—alone or entertaining? Or, do they prefer public socializing, such as restaurants/bars, sports events, travel?

Sizes: (for clothes and accessories)

Color preferences: (Include color dislikes, too).

Other: Include current needs and interests, or projects that are of a temporary nature.

GIFTING RIGHT

TRACKING IDEA #4:   Remembering Dates — Only 12 Cards

An easy way to remember dates is to have them recorded for easy reference each month.

Using 12 index cards, mark each of the twelve months on separate cards. Or, if you have a Rolodex on your desk, do the same with 12 Rolodex cards. The index cards can fit in a drawer, purse or briefcase. The Rolodex cards can be "filed" in front of the "A" section.

Even if you have dates written by each of your friends' names in an address book, it's easier to remember important dates if you check month by month. You can quickly know what dates are coming up by flipping through only twelve cards.

For each card, write in the name of the month. Write names as you think of them. List the dates as you learn them.

Each number will indicate birthdays unless otherwise noted. If someone has a birthday on January 6, write down "6—Mary Smith." You can squeeze in all 30 or so days, 1,2,3,4,5,6,etc., or else do it the easy way: just write in the number (day) as needed.

Put the year of birth in parentheses. Noting the base year will help you calculate major anniversaries and birthdays—5th, 10th, 25th, 50th.

With only 12 cards, you can quickly and easily see—in advance—if any special events will come up the following month. So, only once a month or every two months, you can review the upcoming important events, then, make a note in your daily appointment book or things-to-do list, so you can get a card, a gift or arrange an event.

THE ORGANIZERS

The Rolodex cards might look like this:

All dates refer to birthdays unless otherwise noted.

If a birthday or other important date is worth remembering, you probably don't need to spell out last names.

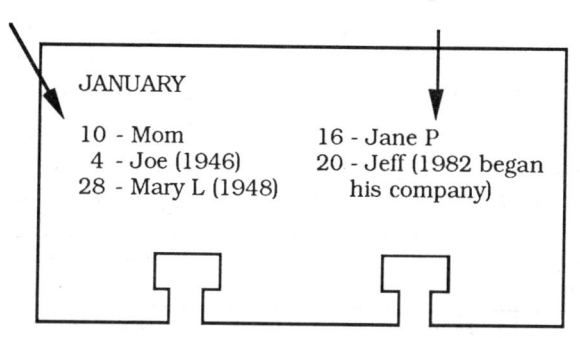

```
JANUARY

10 - Mom              16 - Jane P
 4 - Joe (1946)       20 - Jeff (1982 began
28 - Mary L (1948)         his company)
```

Put year of wedding, birthday or other such date as soon as you learn it, so you can figure when 5, 10, 25 years are coming

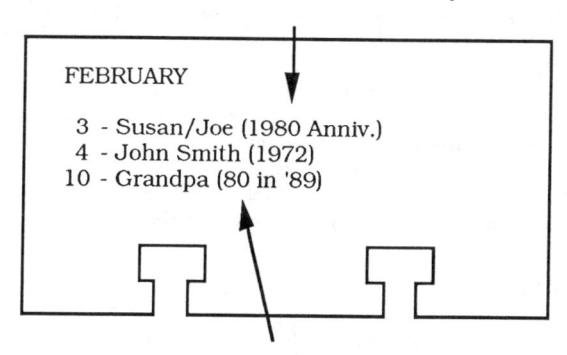

```
FEBRUARY

 3 - Susan/Joe (1980 Anniv.)
 4 - John Smith (1972)
10 - Grandpa (80 in '89)
```

Or note when the next big birthday or anniversary will occur.

TRACKING IDEA #5: Know Your Gift Giving Needs For An Entire Year & Other Organization Tips

How many gifts will you buy this year? Ten? Twenty? Fifty? How much will you spend? Do you need to budget?

By estimating your gift giving needs during the coming year, you will know how much to spend, or budget. You also will have the added benefit of being able to quickly "assign" great gift ideas as you spot them throughout the year.

GIFTING RIGHT

On the following page is a chart to help you figure out how many gifts or cards you wish to get and for whom. If you have lots of gifts to get throughout the year, xerox a separate sheet for each category—family, friends and co-workers. If you have other associations (religious, community service, hobby group), you may wish to use a separate sheet for each of those as well. It will be easier to add names and make changes.

Names	Jan	Feb	Mar	Apr	May	Jun	Jul	Aug	Sep	Oct	Nov	Dec	Budget
Mom					14							H	$50
Dad	3											H	$50
Vicki										11		H	$15
Jeff	5											H	$15
Liz								9				H	$15
Wendy		22										H	$15
Gannon						17						H	$15
Bob					A-4							H	$25
Cissel			A-2				10					H	$20
Boss												H	$30
Secret												H	$35

How to use the chart: A number means an event occurs that month and you wish to get a gift or card. You may also put a "B" for birthday or "A" for anniversary. An "H" in the December column means you'll get a holiday gift. In the budget column, estimate what you want to spend that year, and add it all up to learn if you need to tighten your belt with gifts. Or, determine your annual gift budget, then divide it up among the people you wish to give gifts and cards.

Summary

If you understand the gift selection process, you do not have to spend a lot of unpleasant time mulling over gift choices. If you are organized, you will save more time, make gift decisions earlier, and give a truly appreciated gift! With the quick and easy record keeping in this chapter, anyone can take advantage of the great gift ideas found from a variety of sources throughout the year, know where to find them when you need them, and remember to use them before it's too late.

The Organizers

Names	Jan	Feb	Mar	Apr	May	Jun	Jul	Aug	Sep	Oct	Nov	Dec	Budget

For your use. Xerox a separate sheet each for family, friends and co-workers.

SEVEN

TEN EXTRA TIPS THAT WRAP IT UP

1. Buy ahead.

Accumulate quality gift items, large and small. By doing so, you'll have your own gift shop of items to choose from for any occasion that suddenly appears or one you were unable to prepare for. It might be a wedding of the not-well-known son or daughter of a business colleague, or you may want a hostess gift for a last-minute dinner invitation.

When buying far in advance, if you do not have a specific person in mind, don't buy something too exotic, no matter how great a bargain it is. You may end up keeping it forever, because you may never figure out who would want it. You should accumulate these carefully and sparingly, so you don't end up with a closet full of items never given. That's another reason you will be happier stocking items that you personally like or would use. Also check with Chapter 8 "Generic Gifts" for ideas of products that adapt to almost every occasion and person.

If you locate a "perfect" gift for a friend or relative many months ahead of their birthday or other occasion, get it! Don't think "what if something better comes along later on..." If it does, give both!

Pay attention to sales. Buying ahead when there are sales, is a particularly good idea for big-cost items, such as wedding gifts. In addition to spreading out the cost of gift items throughout the year, you can give someone a more expensive, better quality item than your budget allows. If you can only afford to spend $20 on a gift, wouldn't it be nice to present an item that was worth $40, $50 or more? You will be able to find $10 picture frames for $5, $40 candlesticks for $20, or $500 silver-plated tea sets for $150, by watching for sales. And even more incredible savings can be found at "Going Out Of Business" sales!

2. Avoiding The Agony of Gift Giving.

Let's face it. Some people are hard-to-please, but for a variety of reasons we are obligated to give them gifts.

It's not worth agonizing over the gift selection any more than you have to for these hard-to-please folks. They are not going to change. Just take your best shot at a clever, practical or classy gift. If you cannot afford to spend a lot pleasing these difficult folks, get one-of-a-kind gifts or create a unique "package." Determine if they want a quality or sensational gift—a case of fine wines, crystal candlesticks, a bouquet of balloons or "happy birthday" spray-painted on their front lawn or car (washable, of course). If they're really tough to please, get fancy foods or wines; maybe they'll get all choked up.

3. Pay attention to the quality of products and the materials they are made of.

Buy quality over quantity if the recipient will notice the difference. If your budget is limited, and you know the recipient(s) favor a high quality lifestyle and expensive possessions, give a *small* high quality gift than a "bigger" gift of lesser quality. It's better to buy a modest gift at a store known for high quality, or items of quality material (silver or leather, rather than metal or vinyl), than to get a medium quality gift just because it looks more substantial. Good things do come in small packages. A male executive told me he would rather get one $10 linen cotton handkerchief than the lesser quality even though one can get 6 handkerchiefs for $12. To add pizazz, tie up the one great quality handkerchief with a balloon or fresh flowers!

GIFTING RIGHT

4. Check Out Garage Sales.

This is a wonderful source to locate unusual gifts. You can often find high quality/like-new items at a fraction of the cost a store would charge—and sometimes valuable antiques or art at a "steal".

5. The Yellow Pages.

If your city does not have the most up-to-date, trendy or fully stocked shops, look in *The Yellow Pages* (found in most public libraries) of a nearby major city. You can often order by phone or mail. Many shops have catalogs and would be glad to send one to a potential customer.

6. Upgrade the Quality.

If you have a choice, buy the upgraded version of any product. And also remember, that although the recipient of your gift already has a certain product, he or she may appreciate being presented with the higher quality version.

7. Giving to Acquaintances.

For those you don't know well, give functional or consumable gifts rather than decorative gifts. The "generic" gift list works well. Also, if there are a variety of styles from which to choose, it's safest to select a plain or classic style.

8. Ask sales personnel for suggestions.

Sales personnel know the stock better than you, so they might give you a great idea or lead you to discover items you weren't aware of. If one sales person does not come up with ideas, be patient and try another. You may have gotten someone who is not particularly creative (or as "brilliant" as you would be if you worked there), even if they know the merchandise.

9. "It's the thought that counts."

There's a reason for the above oft-quoted saying. The dollar amount is really unimportant to real friends. It's your effort that counts, taking the time to get or create a personalized gift—something really wanted or extremely important to the person—or giving of your time as the gift. In fact, sending a card (carefully selected, of course) with a personal message may hit the spot perfectly.

10. Brainstorm.

Talk with friends, colleagues or family for ideas. Or, settle into a comfortable chair, relax, and review the following *Gifting Right*, ideas—because, with no stress, you will find the perfect gift!

THE LISTS

EIGHT

GENERIC GIFTS

34 Items That Adapt To Any Person, Occasion Or Budget

The items that follow are "generic" because they are needed or used by almost every person at one time or another and can be found anywhere, in large and small cities. They also are suitable for almost every occasion and can be adapted to different ages and lifestyles.

Because they can be found in different styles, designs and materials, their prices vary enormously making them adaptable to any budget.

They are listed in alphabetical order for ease of reference and are not based on any value. Headings serve as an umbrella for *types* of gifts. For example, "Address Books," refer to all sorts of items that may fall into that category, such as phones with number memory or pocket computers with name-number listings.

ADDRESS BOOKS—Everyone organizes their friends or business colleagues' names in some way. Therefore, address books can be used and found in homes, offices, pockets or handbags. A small purse-size, fabric or vinyl covered address book can be found at a Five-and-Dime or department store for a teenage girl's birthday gift. High quality leather-covered address books found at fine stationery, leather goods or gift shops can be presented for a housewarming, office or wedding gift.

Names and addresses can be organized in forms other than books. In offices, addresses and telephone numbers are often organized on a Rolodex, which come in many sizes and styles, from plastic, leather or brass to the finest woods and other materials, often designed to match all desk accessories to give one's desk a coordinated look.

The Lists

If someone already has an address book or Rolodex, consider *upgrading* theirs—replacing a plastic Rolodex with a wood or bronze version—or *replacing* a worn and doggy-eared address book of the same model, if the quality is already tops, like fine leather.

You might consider presenting as part of the gift, the offer (by you perhaps?) to transcribe all the names, addresses and phone numbers, from the old book to the new. Now, wouldn't that be a treat for anyone?

APPOINTMENT BOOKS/ORGANIZERS—Like address books, these also come in different sizes and with many types of covers—in leather, or in fabrics with lively patterns and colors. They can be presented for formal or informal occasions depending on the quality of the product. Since they are used in home, office or on the road, you can adapt them to any lifestyle.

Some people organize their schedule using only a pocket size appointment book with each page showing an entire week or month. Some need a page for every day to keep track, especially in professions that require a dozen or more appointments or meetings daily. Others may find it more practical to keep track of appointments or special occasions by using a massive wall chart. (See "calendars" on next page).

The latest versions of the appointment book are "organizers" that, in addition to calendars, include sections to organize your thoughts, menus and grocery lists, friends' birthdays and addresses, and whatever else you can think of, all into one notebook or loose leaf. With the many variations of appointment books nowadays, you can find just the one to suit your giftee's needs.

BOOKS—There are books on every subject, for every taste and age. You can find large art or photo books ("coffee table books"), or books on cooking, humor or religion, history, general reference, self-help and how-to books. There are even blank books for the budding author, poet or recipe collector. Books are accessible in the U.S. everywhere—even drug stores, newsstands and grocery stores. Many "remaindered" and discount book shops have mushroomed in recent years, giving us accessibility to more quality-looking books, more economically. Or, how about a book called *"Gifting Right?"*

BOOKENDS—Bookends can be used by young children, college students or business executives. Children's shops usually carry colorful rainbow or cheery animal bookends. Specialty or gift shops may have bookends designed to reflect one's hobby or profession. Brass, marble or leather bookends can also be found for the home (living room or bedroom) or the office of the most successful business executive or inspired student. Office supply stores are another source for traditional, conservative bookends or cheery, bright-colored models. Also, visit antique shops for unique or one-of-a-kind bookends.

CALENDARS—The range is wide for this category for suiting all tastes and interests. Humorous or male/female "art" calendars, or those with exquisite reproductions of museum art or photographs, can be hung on the wall or placed on a desk, in a kitchen, office or in a child's bedroom. Perennial calendars, also, can be found in silver frames at antique or jewelry shops, or fine goods shops or department stores that carry frames or desk accessories.

CANDY—Whether it's candy canes, a bag of Hershey's kisses or lemon drops, fine imported chocolates or "jelly bellies," you can always present candy with pleasing results.

If fancy imported chocolates are not appropriate or available, wrap up small candies from Five-and-Dime stores. If you make it amusing, your gift will make a great impression. If certain candies have a special, personal meaning to the Giftee—such as "penny" candies for the child within—they are indeed high quality as a gift.

If you want something more exotic, and expensive, locate fine confectioners or chocolatiers in major cities. Some shops have shaped chocolate into everything from single alphabet letters, to tennis rackets or a woman's bust. If they are not available where you live, locate a shop in a major city and get the information by mail or telephone. Look under "confectioners" in *The Yellow Pages* of major cities. (Note—public libraries often have *The Yellow Pages* for most major U.S. cities).

The Lists

CARDS—There are many occasions when you don't need to give a gift, but you want to acknowledge the occasion and honor a person. That's where cards do the trick. There are cards for every sentiment and occasion. But, on the rare occasion you can't find one or haven't had time to card shop, make your own note. It will be appreciated.

CASH—Cash is often the best type of Christmas gift for service personnel—hairdressers, maintenance staff, gardeners or garage attendants. When in doubt about obligatory year-end gifts, turn to cash, because cash will always be appreciated. (If you're not sure about the amount to give, ask friends, colleagues, other customers or neighbors. Listen to their suggestions and then adapt their suggested amount with your good instincts and what you can afford). Get cash envelopes from banks or at greeting card racks. Or present the cash in personal stationery envelopes or with holiday greeting cards, adding a personal note if you wish, although a simple "Thanks" and signing your name, gets the message across.

CERTIFICATES—The best gift certificates are **individually created** for the occasion and person. Some people might consider gift certificates boring or "the easy way out." True sometimes, but not if you use your imagination.

Certificates are handy when you don't know a person's *specific* tastes, just their general interests. For example, a cash certificate to a record store would be gladly put to use by a teenager; as it would be at an ice cream parlor for a younger child.

For adults, look at certificates as a way of *contributing to necessary or splurge expenses*. A coupon book for two tickets to the theater, sports event or concert, or four deluxe, brushless car washes, for example. **Be as specific as possible**. What about arranging with a restaurant a pre-paid dinner for two, or a bottle of fine wine or champagne. Then give as a gift a note that says "To Mary and John....This entitles you to a bottle of champagne at Cafe Sorbonne."

Or consider giving adults a certificate for a special dessert or specialty item prepared at a nearby restaurant, a carry-out shop or delicatessen. How could one resist having the opportunity to taste a famous and delicious food item—from freshly-made pesto sauce to chestnut ice cream or lobster bisque. What food item is the rage in your locality?

Fit the certificate to match the person's interests as closely as possible. A certificate personally fashioned by you should fit the person's wants or needs perfectly. Money certificates are not impersonal if you have targeted it to the recipient's personal needs or interests.

A cash gift certificate to a department store may not seem clever, *but* if the person is elderly, lives near the store and is not highly mobile, *and* you don't know exactly what he or she needs, it is a fine gift. If the person is more active, direct that money elsewhere. Make it fun by giving the person an excuse to visit a new shop or location. Or, give them a certificate to a store you know they love—and add to it by arranging transportation.

Certificates are better the more specific you can be—a specific store, a specific amount, a specific item. For example, if you have a friend who you witnessed admiring wool scarves at a certain store, for her birthday, you can pick up an individually-designed certificate at that store for the exact amount of that type of scarf (plus tax). Present it with a note (or a card) that her gift is "the wool scarf at X shop in the color of her choice." Not only does she have the fun of selecting the color that best fits into her wardrobe, she will also appreciate the gift because she knew her friend was paying attention when she admired those scarves.

Ask the shop to adapt the exact amount you wish to spend. Some shops only offer pre-printed cash certificates of *even*-dollar amounts or multiples of five or ten. Don't let it box you in, if you think it's more fun and appropriate to give another amount. Ask the shop if they have blank gift certificates so you can write in your own figure. If not, talk them into using any paper with their official letterhead. The gift language can then be personally hand-written or typed. *Be sure to get the signature of someone in authority*—the manager not a sales clerk—so the personalized, non-traditional certificate is not questioned when your friend shows up with it later.

The Lists

Be creative when figuring the amount of the certificate. After you figure out generally how much you want to spend, determine if you can adapt the dollars and cents to the current year, the receiver's birthday, anniversary or occasion of the event, his or her address, or any other special date or number. Here's how to do it. If you wish to spend about $10 and the person was born on October 21 (10/21) purchase a certificate for $10.21. Play with numbers to come up with the amount you wish to spend. Juggle with the date of the event, a birth date, one's age, their street number or the year. If you are giving a gift in 1991, instead of getting an even $20 certificate at a prestigious gourmet food shop, ask for a certificate made out for "$19.91." Personally-designed cash gift certificates are definitely more fun and less bland to give and to receive! Even if the shop has to write up a certificate on blank letterhead, ask! It shows the giftee that you made a special effort for them.

CLOCKS/WATCHES—Clocks are used everywhere. Travel alarm clocks. Clock radios. Formal living room clocks. Wall clocks for kitchen or office. Think of every room in the person's life. What are their habits? For someone that travels frequently, get a wristwatch that shows what time it is overseas. Or would he or she prefer a colorful modern clock or a formal, classic table clock in a wood grained case? How about a Mickey Mouse wristwatch, or one of the new plastic wristwatches that come in a rainbow of colors and designs? Or, perhaps, you can afford to give a gold watch for day and a jeweled watch for night. There are clocks and watches in every price range and style to suit anyone's taste or needs.

CLOTHES/ACCESSORIES—You must, of course, know the person's interests or lifestyle fairly well to be most successful. Start with someone's head and work your way down to their toes. If you don't want to get clothes, consider accessories. Hats, socks, scarves, belts, sweaters and rings. Which accessory would you be comfortable giving them? Clothes and accessories reflect one's identity so you must know what you are doing (i.e., know the person well) for your gift to be a hit. Remember that if you and the person have different tastes, get something he or she would like and wear, not because you like it. Also, the depth of relationship is reflected in clothes as a present; lingerie is a marvelous present from a husband or close friend. It is not appropriate from a casual office mate.

COCKTAIL NAPKINS—Cocktail napkins range from fancy engraved monogrammed linens suitable for weddings to pre-packaged paper cocktail napkins with humorous or apt sayings, great for a hostess gift or any occasion "just because."...Stationers that engrave wedding invitations also can engrave napkins, but they do not always offer the widest or most creative selections. Check with party shops that will engrave paper napkins in any message or initials of your choice, sometimes in colors matching the person's living room, party room, boat or backyard! Buy napkins or other paper products separately and bring them to a print house if you must, but...Personalize! Personalize!

DECORATIVE ACCESSORIES—Any house can use more than one of the true generic home accessories. Think of each room in the house and how each is used. What is on the tables, floors, walls? A **vase, frame** or **candlesticks** are good gifts because it's always nice to have more than one. A small silver or china candy **dish** can be used for keys at the front door or for pocket change on your bedroom bureau, not just candy. You might even put a different kind of candy in the dish when you present it, such as penny candies to evoke nostalgia. Other items to be considered are **lamps, umbrella stands, magazine racks** or **coat hooks. Lighting wall switchplates** in brass, ceramic or wood, or **doorknockers** will require that you first know the person's house needs. So, these are not generic gifts for many "acquaintances."

But always, if you do not know the person's lifestyle and tastes and interests, definitely choose a simple classic style or design. Find out enough about someone's lifestyle to know if they prefer higher quality items or not. For the label conscious, it's better to get a tiny $20 china dish or ashtray from Tiffany & Co. than a $20 teapot from a moderately-priced department store.

DESK ACCESSORIES—Fine pens, engraved pencils, leather or brass frames, a vase with silk flowers, a potted plant, an appointment book. What about a box of No. 2 pencils or an electric pencil sharpener? If the person would appreciate it,

THE LISTS

get it! Go to stationers, department stores, or fine leather goods shops which usually carry an array of desk accessories. But don't overlook Five & Dime stores, office supply shops, or lamp shops. Include paper products found at these shops. Also, museum shops carry paper products such as note pads, frames and address books, usually with exquisite coverings of hand painted designs or reproductions of art works.

Ask yourself, what goes on a desk, near a desk or in an office? A lamp, chair, poster, print or barometer are just as appropriate as a letter opener, pen and appointment calendar. Repeat to yourself...what does the person want? What does the person need? What will the person use?

DINING ACCESSORIES—Mentally walk through your friend's dining room, kitchen, living room as they might entertain. What utensils would they use? How would they serve their food? With paper plates in the summer and fine china in the winter? Knowing these facts would determine their formality. The nice thing about serving pieces is that they are often both practical and attractive, and found everywhere. Serving spoons, forks or knives for cakes, vegetables or meats, can be located at local housewares shops, department stores, antique shops or flea markets. Napkin rings are also easy to find (or make) and adapt easily to a wide variety of tastes because they can be made of sterling silver, straw flowers or playful animal figures. Placemats or table cloths should also be considered for formal or informal selections.

FOOD—Gourmet delicacies or everyday foods. Pre-packaged or put together by you. A variety of food gifts can be presented:

(1) *For a college student*—A care package sent by mail must not include anything that would spoil without refrigeration or be damaged or broken in transit. A sample care package might contain homemade cookies, a box of brownie or cake mix, if the student has a kitchen (include a pan if you know that's lacking), beef jerky, candy bars, dried fruits, cashews or other nuts, and a book of stamps or self-addressed stamped envelopes or postcards to ensure you will hear from the person.

(2) *For a newly married couple*—Champagne and caviar to celebrate their love and marriage, as well as a jar of gourmet popcorn for two people who will undoubtedly enjoy staying at home.

(3) *For a family who has just moved into a new neighborhood*—food products from popular local stores they should know about, or offer samples of the food representative of that city or region.

(4) *For a best friend*—an assortment of food or utensils so one can enjoy their favorite cuisine (for those less talented in the kitchen get food that is already prepared). Sushi lovers could get rice and rice vinegar, seaweed, wasabi, bamboo roll, a certificate for fresh fish at the local fish market, and, perhaps, sake cups and carafe. Italian food fiends would love a selection of home-made pastas, pesto and marinara sauces, freshly-ground Parmesan and maybe even a pasta-making machine.

(5) *A sick friend*—Whatever the doctor will allow. If the doctor has prescribed a limited diet, present items the patient can enjoy after she has recuperated, such as champagne, chocolate chip cookies, or an invitation for dinner at her favorite restaurant.

(6) *An elderly person who lives alone*—Get his or her favorite treats, but respect his or her diet if it is limited. Candy, ice cream, nuts, fruits, vegetables, meats or fish. Bring him or her a home-made entree, or two, that can be heated up.

FRAMES—Frames are the most versatile of gifts. One can find frames in any size and material, from silver, leather, or cloissone to fabric, paper or plastic, with designs or without, with one opening, two or more. There are even portable frames which enable people to bring photos of their loved ones on trips. They are often designed in paper or leather because these materials are light in weight and are crush-proof. If you are looking for a gift for a young girl or lady, remember that a locket also is a "portable" frame.

As with all gifts, where there is a choice it's better to get a small quality frame than a larger inexpensive frame. However,

The Lists

if your major gift is the photograph or insert* *in* the frame, and you have a limited budget, select a frame with a plain design, because a carefully chosen frame can look more expensive than it is. Also, for those of you looking for quality on a budget, don't overlook moderately-priced department or catalog stores such as Sears-Roebuck which have good-looking brass or silver-plated frames in basic styles and will save you money without sacrificing quality, especially if your photograph requires a large frame. Remember, the higher priced shops do have quality items, but part of the higher price you pay is for their exclusive and reputable name.

> **Frame inserts*—Consider photographs of family, friends, scenes from past or present, including friends or sites (buildings, cities). Frame certificates, as well as something you've written—a poem or informal note. Also consider humorous photos and cartoons. The Giftee doesn't need to keep the insert in the frame, but it adds to a marvelous presentation.

GLASSES—There are glasses for every type of liquid and as formal or informal as one wishes. If friends have a good stock of basic glasses, consider adding something they might not have or buy themselves—extra wine glasses, old-fashioned, liqueur or brandy glasses. Would they enjoy getting more crystal glasses like Waterford or prefer pottery coffee mugs? For a wedding night, present two distinctive champagne glasses. Maybe it would be more appreciated to replenish a young family's stock of everyday drinking glasses. Or glasses for summer get togethers (tall, frosted ice tea glasses) or a friend's boat or poolside (attractive plastic tumblers)?

If you believe the glasses by themselves are not "enough," consider presenting the liquid that goes with your choice of glasses, or put a flower or piece of candy (i.e., a chocolate Hershey's kiss?) in each glass.

LAMPS—Lamps can be formal and expensive for a living room. There are also reading lamps for home or student dormitories. Children, too, might enjoy a cheerful lamp with balloons or airplanes. Flashlights, too, are lamps for inside or outside the home.

LESSONS—Contribute your expertise in the form of a gift certificate—"Five tennis lessons." "Enough sewing sessions to help complete a dress." Or "assistance in baking bread." See the section on presenting the gift of "Time," which soon follows.

LIQUEURS/LIQUORS—Fine liqueurs, a 12-year-old scotch, or cognac—those that *last more than one sitting*—are appropriate for birthdays, as house gifts or for second weddings. In England, for example, a case of vintage port is given as a christening present to be held as a trust for the child's 21st birthday. You could vary this tradition by giving a bottle of excellent vintage, young wine given as a wedding gift, to be consumed on a 5th, 10th or 20th anniversary. (Also, see "wine," following). If you give more than one bottle, a bottle of champagne or wine—which can be *emptied in one sitting*—can be added for variety. Ask liquor store owners for suggestions about combinations based on your friend's tastes and lifestyles, and your budget.

ORGANIZERS—There are organizers for just about everything. Mentally walk through every room in your friend's house or apartment, or walk through their day to determine what he or she might find useful. There are organizers for paper (letters, messages, files), for pens, pencils, paper clips and other desk accessories, for magazines, cosmetics, jewelry or videocassettes; for kitchen utensils or food; for the bathroom, for a car; for the closet; or travel organizers for vacations or taking to the health club or gym.

PARTIES—Parties are gifts, too—whether a lunch or dinner for six to a large festive bash for one hundred. By arranging a party, you are giving your time which is a most precious gift. And if you think a larger party would make the Giftee most happy, but you can't afford it, ask friends to contribute. And not just money. Ask for their time, too. Most people will enjoy the opportunity to participate in the celebration of a friend. And if you are not naturally creative about gifts or parties, brainstorm with friends and recruit those who you know will have lots of ideas.

PENS, PENCILS—Pens can be given to students, graduates, those starting out in business or successful executives. A pen can seem like a dull gift until one realizes the range they come in. Mont Blanc fountain pens can cost $250, and unless it

The Lists

would be appreciated, it would not be a logical present for just anyone. But, what is true for all gifts, is that success depends on matching the person and the occasion to your relationship with that person. Inexpensive disposable felt-tip or ballpoint pens or pencils might be perfect gifts, especially if you gave an entire box of 12 or 20. There are also very fine pens that can be presented individually. They might include a gold-filled Cross pen, an engraved silver pen or other expensive pens or pencils found in specialty shops such as fine gift and leather shops that often carry desk accessories. Department, stationery and catalog stores often have nice selections for a variety of pens and prices. Large cities feature shops that specialize in writing utensils alone. Check in *The Yellow Pages*.

PHOTOGRAPHS—Any photo that conjures up positive and special feelings in someone would make a great gift. It could be one of the photos you have taken—formal or candid. On the other hand, you may decide to engage a professional photographer or have an artist draw a picture from a photograph.

It's your choice as to how to present it—what size, by itself or framed. Rather than presenting one photo in a frame, you may wish to compile many in a photo album and present the entire book. What about pasting photos in a scrap book with your own captions? The varieties of gifts that include photos are endless. Pick the photo(s) first and see where your mind wanders, or brainstorm with one or two people to figure out how best to present the photos—to make them look elegant, sentimental, or as humorous as possible!

RADIOS—Radios can be found everywhere and they are used by almost everyone everywhere—in the car or home—even in the shower. Portable ones are made for walking, exercising, commuting or travelling. Some radios' additional functions enhance their use so substantially that they change from just being radios—such as a clock radio or as part of a stereo system at home or in the car.

STATIONERY—Stationery can range from 25-cent note cards to fine engraved stationery worth hundreds of dollars. Therefore, it is easy to find something for everyone in the stationery category. But, one should keep a few things in mind before selecting stationery as a gift.

Stationery reflects the image of the writer, so get stationery you are confident the person would realistically use, not just because you like it.

Flowered note cards are perfect for some, but solid colored note cards and envelopes may be the better choice for others. Some others might prefer a box of plain white note cards from a fine stationer. The formality of the stationery, of course, depends on the lifestyle of the person.

Just try to match the person's personality and lifestyle. Use your best instincts. Ask yourself if someone would prefer something colorful or conservative, note cards or letter paper, with their name imprinted or left blank?

SUBSCRIPTIONS—Again, there is something here for everyone. Even widely circulated weekly news magazines are good gifts if a personal subscription is a welcome splurge to the beneficiary. There are plenty of specialty and trade magazines that also might be greatly appreciated by others— *Consumer Reports, Crocheting, Photography, National Geographic, Sports Illustrated, Reader's Digest* in Spanish or other languages, *Vogue, Working Women,* computer-related and magazines for specific cities.

There are also a number of magazines that cater to teenagers or children. Children would enjoy getting something in the mail on a regular basis. Check with the child's school or local public library for ideas. Or consider publications the kids may have brought home.

TIME—The most personalized gift you can give is your time—the time you spend to locate a marvelous gift or your time as the gift itself. For example:

15 Hours Of Babysitting

One Massage—(If you have the knack, do it yourself. It may not be as thorough as a professional massage, but I doubt you will get a complaint).

A Catered Meal for six; hor d'heurves for 30

The Lists

A Lesson In How To Needlepoint, Play Tennis, or Drive A Car

A Haircut

The categories are unlimited. **If you have a special talent, put it to use** as a personalized gift. As the section on "Lessons" above suggests, teach the person about something for which you have a talent. Also consider presenting the services of others in the service industry as the gift—haircut, gardening, piano tuning. See the list of "Services" in Chapter Nine.

Also, consider doing errands for people, especially the elderly or ill. Offer to drive someone to the grocery store every month. Or take someone who lives alone to the movies or theater.

TRAYS—Trays are used for perfume or carrying anything that needs to be carried in the home, such as food or serving pieces. Some exquisite models can be used more for decoration than function. You can find them in all price ranges, because they are made in everything from plastic and bamboo to mirrors, silver and hand-carved wood. Pick a hand crafted tray on a trip to an exotic land or a florentine tray from Florence, Italy. Or locate a unique tray at a flea market or antique dealer. Get a smaller tray for use in the front hall for keys, or on the bedroom bureau for coins and cuff links, or, why not a bed tray?

WINE—One bottle can be presented or a full case, depending on the person and the occasion, since wines come in the finest vintages to everyday table wine. One bottle can be presented even for a wedding gift, if it is high quality, vintage wine, to be consumed on the fifth or tenth anniversary. Otherwise, for good everyday wines, a full or half case would be more appropriate for major events. One bottle, however, of whatever quality you can afford is a fine gift for dinner hosts.

NINE

GIFT SOURCES TO USE NEAR HOME OR FAR AWAY

Overlooked Sources

There are numerous gift-locating resources that should not be overlooked. They include specialty shops, public libraries, magazines and catalogs. With these tools you will consistently locate and present uniquely personal and appreciated gifts for all ages. Sources for gift ideas include:

Hardware stores
Nails, paint and plaster compounds are not the only items at hardware stores. Functional and decorative house fixtures can be found, especially at the larger hardware stores. Lighting fixtures, kitchen gadgets and door knockers are there. If you want a functional gag gift, go to a well-stocked hardware or do-it-yourself home furnishing store, and be inspired. Presenting a large quantity of everyday items, which by themselves would be insignificant, could be the hit of the party!

Book shops
There are books for every interest and personality, and in addition, many book stores stock other items, such as art calendars, address books, notecards and pens, and sometimes more.

Office supply stores
These stores have everything and more for organizing all the paper and office supplies in your office or home—files and file labels, notepads of every size and color, and calendars. Some also stock decorative items that can be used at office or home. Consider giving stock items to children as gifts: colored pens and pencils; ticket coupons to entice them to produce a neighborhood event or show; or accounting ledger paper and invoice forms, so they can learn to run a business. Put together a selection of individual items. Tied together or put into a larger box or container is a great gift!

The Lists

Sporting goods shops
Exercise equipment, good-looking, warm and durable indoor and outdoor clothes, gloves, hats, socks, boots, slippers, long underwear, heavy sweaters, parkas, coats; sporting equipment and many small items that are functional or fun—compass, flashlight, freeze-dried food. Mail order catalogues from the likes of Eddie Bauer and L.L. Bean allow us all to shop from home.

Toy stores
You will get plenty of ideas and gifts for kids, but don't overlook toy stores for the child within the adult. Monopoly, scrabble, dominoes or stuffed animals, paint sets and bicycles are just a beginning.

Gift, novelty and card shops
Besides cards, you will find a larger quantity of less functional items at these shops. A good place to go for gifts for the office, friends or the person who has fewer "needs." Look in *The Yellow Pages* under "gifts" or "gift shops." Specialty gift shops often have advertisements in *The Yellow Pages* which describe their unique offerings; and may give you great ideas, too. Many of these are found in shopping malls and carry hot, new, trendy items!

Artists' studios
For the person who has everything, consider commissioning an amateur or professional artist's services to paint or draw a portrait of the person, his or her spouse, children or parents, house, pet, or other treasured possession.

In addition to traditional paintings, think about items that are handmade. Is there a craftsman who can make a handbag or jewelry? How about etching someone's name, a special message or a picture of a favorite pet or possession on a crystal vase or in needlepoint?

Special Talents, Gifts By You—If you are an artist or craftsman, giving friends and relatives your works will usually be greatly appreciated. And throughout the years, it could become your trademark to give personally crafted gifts.

Public libraries
Gift ideas about home-made gifts and food items, and decorations, can be found in books at the local library. Magazines, also, will have gift ideas. Look under "gifts" in the Reader's Guide or ask the reference librarian for assistance.

Magazines/newspapers advertisements
Advertisements share many new and refreshing ideas for gifts—especially during the months before Christmas. Periodicals gear the products or services advertised to the readers. For example, *the Wall Street Journal* advertises products suitable for executives. Glance at the advertisements or products pushed by specialty consumer and trade magazines for additional suggestions if your friend has a specific hobby or interest, from *Boating* to *Psychology Today*.

Institutions, sites or products indigenous to a city, country or region

In your travels, or where you live, what does that city or country have that no one else has? Items related to regions and their local institutions would be unique gifts to those who live in other cities or countries.

Institutions—In Washington, D.C. there is the White House, the Capitol, and the Smithsonian Institution. In England, there is the Tower of London, Buckingham Palace and more. In Italy, there is Vatican City, as well as Milan and Florence, fashion and art capitals of the world. All have specialized memento shops.

In addition to typical souvenir items, like a miniature Statue of Liberty, consider getting "functional" souvenirs. These items can be just as much fun and do more than serve as dust collectors. They are not impossible to find. Coffee mugs with the insignia or the name of the home city make practical souvenirs. Even small commemorative dishes can double as ashtrays or a place for jewelry, coins or bobby pins. Note pads, address books, pens or letter openers, with the institution's or city's recognizable emblem or logo are also useful.

The Lists

Museum shops
Many museums have gift shops. Among souvenirs, one can find unique, quality items, as well as T-shirts, statues, postcards and coffee mugs that convey "I thought of you while on my trip." Traditionally we go to museums on vacations or weekends and although we might pick up some gifts then, we don't always consider *looking* there specifically for a gift.

In museums one can find jewelry and hand-crafted decorative pieces for the home—often the crafts are indigenous to the area or the theme of that particular museum, adding to the uniqueness of the item as a gift. For that reason, inexpensive quality gifts can be found, as well as one-of-a-kind items. Even at our finest art museum shops, one can find inexpensive address books or note pads covered in classic designs or reproductions of art masterpieces.

The Smithsonian museum shops in Washington, D.C. are chock-full of jewelry, scarves, books, toys, gadgets, educational toys, as well as decorative household gifts. The Museum of Natural History has three-dimensional models of dinosaurs and the Air and Space Museum stocks toys and books on space travel. Each museum has items designed to the specific theme in addition to general interest items. Since you can often find items unique to that city or region, museum shops are also great places to find gifts for those who don't live nearby.

The Metropolitan Museum in New York City, the Smithsonian Institution in Washington, D.C., and other large and small museums have catalogues of their many fine products, so if you aren't able to travel to those or other museums, write or call to request the catalog.

Special exhibits
One-time-only exhibits provide opportunities for unique mementoes. Whether of individual artists, or theme exhibits, you can bring friends a handsome poster, coffee table book or replicas of ancient jewelry or antiques, commemorating the occasion. Sending an attractive postcard representing the exhibit may be sufficient.

There are almost always hoards of inexpensive, but tasteful, souvenirs at museums. For less expensive, but often fun, souvenir gifts, check the wares of the enterprising entrepreneurs *outside* museums who cater to the tourist trade. Here, too, you can get souvenirs that friends back home will appreciate. Just be careful that they are not charging an extraordinary markup and that their authentic products are truly authentic and not "knock-offs."

Local products
Determine if a city is known for a certain type of product or export. Perfume or chocolates? Leather shoes and handbags, or silk scarves? Brass, china or crystal? Don't forget local foods indigenous to the area if you are travelling. Be sure there is no provision against transporting that type of food across state or country borders.

Whatever the popular and plentiful local product, local merchandisers usually stock miniature sizes, specifically for token gifts to friends or office colleagues back home.

Special celebrations
In addition to institutions in certain cities, look at special celebrations as a source of unique gift items.

Expos and other world fairs would be great vehicles for finding unique gifts. Friends or colleagues would get a kick out of having a memento from these or other highly publicized occasions, like the Olympics, or America's Cup Challenge.

Special art exhibits are also great vehicles for gifts.

Hometown nostalgia
Locate products or arrange to get photos or postcards for a scrapbook from the area where a friend grew up or a place where they spent happy moments, whether it was a place they lived or travelled, or even their alma mater.

The Lists

Using Everyday Lists For Ideas

You can use ordinary lists that you come across daily to find ideas. Directories for department stores or *The Yellow Pages* are two types of lists that can help you eliminate lots of confusion by giving you plenty of new and creative gift ideas.

By focusing your attention on the right type of gift through these lists, you will immediately know what type of store will carry those items. And when you walk in the right store, not only will you have saved yourself lots of time, you will be closer to the perfect gift!

Here's a sample list taken from a variety of everyday sources:

Appliances—air conditioners, heating units
Antiques
Antique repairs and refinishing
Apparel—children's and baby clothes—men and women
Art—dealers, galleries
Art needlework
Art restoring
Art supplies
Auto supplies
Beauty aids
Bicycles
Books
Cameras
Camping equipment
Candles
Candy
Carpets
China and glassware
Closet accessories
Cooking utensils
Convalescent aids
Costumes
Engravers
Fabrics
Fireplace equipment
Flowers
Food—bakery goods, cheese, wine, coffee and tea, gourmet treats, fruits and vegetables, health, ice cream, meats, nuts, poultry, seafood
Fountain pens
Framing
Furniture
Garden furniture and figures
Handbags
Hardware
Hats
Hobbies
House painting
Jewelry—antique, custom, discount, repairs
Kitchen accessories

Lamps
Landscaping
Lawn and garden maintenance
Linens
Lingerie
Luggage
Magazines
Maps
Medicine
Monogramming
Musical instruments
Party equipment
Pets

Shoes
Sporting equipment—horseback riding, ice skating, tennis, hunting, fishing, golf, skiing, swimming, and skin diving
Stationery
Stereo equipment
Television
Toys
Uniforms
Watchmakers
Wines and liquors

Services are Gifts Too!

Services can also be presented as gifts. Your local *Yellow Pages* is a place to start to get ideas. Also, look at the classified business services of local magazines and newspapers.

You can present services as certificates from stores or make homemade certificates, such as writing a personal note in a blank card.

Some services that can be given as gifts—in whole or partially—depending on the cost or complexity of the service, are:

Carpenters and other craftsmen—do they need something built? A table, storage cabinet, extra closet, deck or patio?

Caterers

Cleaners—recruit a commercial cleaning company or students to do heavy duty cleaning for elderly or busy friends

Delivery services

Entertainment—musicians, clowns, singing telegrams

Frames for prints—if you know a print has been purchased and needs framing, or perhaps the picture was drawn by someone special, you might help with the cost of getting a customized frame and mat.

The Lists

Fur repairs, storing

Health clubs—annual membership or one-day visit

Interior decorators

Limousine rental

Party planning

Photographers

Piano tuning

Repairs for decorative pieces—furniture, antiques, art

Restaurants

Schools, courses—dancing, music, secretarial, sports, real estate, hobbies.

Tailors

Tickets—for a trip, to a show, sports event, or special exhibit

Travel

Upholstery

(Certificates, which are a perfect way to present services, are described at length as a Generic Gift in Chapter Eight, plus numerous examples are listed in Chapter Twelve).

TEN

FOR THE PERSON WHO HAS EVERYTHING

Some people appear to have everything, or, at least, everything they want. They are most difficult to buy for, but the task is not impossible. These ideas can be helpful for anyone—wealthy or not—who is generally content with his possessions and does not seem to crave more.

To begin getting ideas, look at their interests and lifestyle. Ask friends or colleagues if he or she has any particular projects or current interests. Use the quick profile list in Chapter Three. Then, ask your most creative friends for unique gift ideas. (For formal occasions or for those you don't know intimately, look at the Generic Gifts list for suggestions).

Generally, for the person who has everything, you should present items that are:

THE TOP OF THE LINE FOR ANY PARTICULAR PRODUCT, EVEN COMMON EVERYDAY ITEMS such as fancy wood hangers for home or office. Buy one, or a dozen for the guest closet, or a hundred for one's entire personal clothes closet.

THE BEST OF THE LATEST FADS, TRENDS OR GADGETS—high tech and "adult" or executive toys, either functional or simply outrageous. For the office, home, travel or hobbies.

A REFLECTION OF THE FINE LIFE FOR SOMEONE WHO CAN NOW SIT BACK AND ENJOY THE FRUITS OF ONE'S LABOR. Fine wines, port or brandy, thermal decanters for coffee or water; humidors or cigars; opera glasses; or theater tickets or any high quality or favored foods and beverages. These *consumable* products are good bets for the person with everything because it's very tricky getting something permanent and durable for someone who often has what he or she needs or wants. If you get an exclusive or exotic gourmet food you only need to get one or a few items, a jar of caviar, a whole (smoked) salmon, a fine cognac. Everyday favorite foods

THE LISTS

are successful too. For these you might present larger quantities— i.e., a crate of oranges from Florida; a five gallon tin of gourmet popcorn. The oranges, chocolates, popcorn or mixed nuts, should be of excellent quality or the best of their category, if possible.

Note that many of these gift ideas are *consumables*—food, drinks, theater tickets, because the person with "everything" rarely needs more tangible, durable items.

PERSONALLY DESIGNED OR MADE by you or a professional artist or craftsman. This could include something as simple as a clay dish made by a child, or something directed to the sentiment of the recipient—a photograph of their house, or spouse.

Ask artists for their suggestions—those who sketch or draw, sculptors or writers. Depending on your budget or particular talents, you might present a drawing of the person's current or childhood home, or perhaps a portrait of those they love—a family member or even a favorite pet.

How about a poem or song written for the occasion? If you want to—maybe your budget demands it—write and perform it yourself. If the recipient has a sentimental bone and prefers what comes from the heart, home-made songs or gifts will be appreciated. In addition to songs or poems, consider sending a singing telegram, a bouquet of helium-filled balloons, or a basket of consumables—foods, wine or liquor. (Many companies will deliver throughout the U.S.)

If you have a talent for any craft—now is the time to create a personal gift. Whether it's needlepoint, carpentry, jewelry design or painting, try your hand at making a personal gift. If you can't come up with the design yourself, ask someone else to sketch a design or present ideas.

ART—If not a personally designed or sentimental work of art, present works of art that are investments. Consider a print, oil painting, sculpture, or even custom-made chair in an award-winning design.

GIFTING RIGHT

SERVICES—You can provide the service yourself or pay others to provide services. Examples: Provide a limousine to take someone to a show or drive them to complete their errands. Take someone to dinner or arrange a basket of food for a candlelight dinner or send a couple on a trip or a short fantasy excursion. For more ideas, see services, Chapter Nine.

* * * * *

Persons on a budget can still locate unique items for presentation in the above categories. Wonderful gifts can be found at flea markets or on sale at your favorite shops. But, whether you have limited funds or not, personally created poems, songs or pictures, or just a sentimental note from the heart can be much appreciated by the person "who has everything."

[NOTE: For a more extensive list, see page 192.]

ELEVEN

GIFTS ON A TIGHT BUDGET

Low or No Cost Gifts

Are you often frustrated selecting gifts because you wish you had more money to spend? Don't fret. You can learn to be more creative and successful in your gift choices without spending a fortune. In fact, sometimes without spending a dime! Not all gifts are material items bought at a store or through a catalog. There are gifts that cost nothing but your time. Whether driving a friend to the airport or helping someone elderly with their spring cleaning, you are giving the precious gift of your time. The **Gifting Right** method includes all these gifts.

Throughout **Gifting Right**, you will notice that the words "purchase" and "buy" are rarely used, because the art of gifting right is to "give" not "buy." It's a way of thinking. Even though we know that most gift choices require some expense, you can learn how to create or select a gift that is so perfect and personalized that the expense (or lack of) is irrelevant.

YOUR TIME

You can give of your time in a variety of ways:

Use your expertise to create. If you have a talent or skill, use it to create or produce a gift.

Are you an artist? Draw or paint a picture of the gift recipient's home, pet, children, or other valued subject. Make a similar personalized gift by doing needlework, sculpture or whatever craft applies to you.

Use your expertise to teach. If you have an expertise or hobby, teach the gift recipient "how to." Provide lessons in how to play tennis, how to sew, etc.

Select any skill in which you have confidence, and share it with someone interested in acquiring that skill. Don't

Gifting Right

underestimate your skills. Even if you are not advanced in your skill, you may still be able to give someone a "beginner" lesson or teach one aspect of the skill. For example, you don't have to be Julia Child to teach a child how to bake cakes and cookies, or teach an adult how to prepare a special ethnic meal that you have mastered.

Provide a service. You need not be an expert to help someone with their repairs, chores, or errands. If you are, however, an expert at carpentry, furniture refinishing or gardening, your friend or relative is extra lucky. But remember that simple things such as helping someone with their spring cleaning or mowing their lawn can be a marvelous gift too! If the person doesn't have the money to pay for maids or gardeners, your services will be much appreciated. To start, ask yourself, "what would save them time or money?"

Depending on your own budget, you can either pay for the service or provide it yourself. For example, let's say you presented your friend with a beautiful (bargain!) picture you located at a flea market. If you couldn't afford to purchase a frame, offer to save your friend the cost of labor by going to a frame-it-yourself shop and putting the frame together. Of course, as long as you're at the flea market, look for frames there too! If the frame is larger than your picture, get an inexpensive colored mat to insert in the frame.

Offer to build or repair something around the house. Perhaps get a few friends or relatives to help. Show up in a group with all your tools, all wearing the same brightly-colored T-shirts, hats, or outfits! Not only would your friends appreciate the cleaning, but they would smile broadly and remember that gift for years to come!

For someone without a car or mobility, provide them with your car or drive yourself! Offer to deliver a package, pick up their cleaning or groceries, or drive them around so they can complete their errands more easily.

Wait in line for tickets in demand. A friend presented his sister with tickets to a popular museum exhibit. Although attendance to the exhibit was free, he saved her hours waiting on line to pick up the tickets. Perhaps your friend has time,

The Lists

but is elderly or ill, and needs to wait on line for something less pleasant, such as for setting up a doctor's appointment or picking up a form or information. These gifts of your time will be appreciated.

HOW TO PRESENT INTANGIBLE GIFTS

Certificates.
As is well documented in Chapter Eight, "Generic Gifts," certificates can be fashioned for any person, amount or gift. You can get a blank certificate from an office supply store, or merely write a note on your stationery, stating your intentions. Here are a few examples:

"*For John—On your birthday, I am delighted to offer you three lessons in archery—Sam.*" You might wish to jazz it up by including a real or fake arrow, a small book on archery, or magazine articles on archery. If you really can't spend a dime, *draw* an arrow and target on a homemade card, and get a few books on archery from the public library. (Of course, make a note when the books are due and offer to return them for your friend).

"*For Sharon—On your fifth anniversary, George and I present you with a weekend of babysitting, at a mutually agreed upon time, so you and Andy can take a well-deserved rest and romantic interlude—Love, Mary.*" To present it, you could put the note in a flashy gift-wrapped box and include an inexpensive trinket or toy for their youngster.

"*To Stan—To determine if you really want to play the piano, this birthday wish comes with three piano lessons at a time of your choosing—Bill.*" For this, you could write the birthday note on sheet music paper and include a beginners' book on piano.

TANGIBLE GIFTS

There are numerous gifts that cost little money. The challenge is to present a "substantial" gift, whether you spend $5 or $50. As outlined throughout the book, if your gift sends the right message you are more than halfway there. Also, refer

GIFTING RIGHT

to the ideas in Chapter Five, "The Enhancers" which explain how to make *any* item better and seem more substantial.

Let's say you visit the bridal registry and find the only item within your budget is a bowl for sugar. (Suppose that you could afford one dish of their china but you would rather present a full place setting which you cannot afford). Get the bowl which will be appreciated because *it is what they want*. Then include a personal message and gift of your time. You might take the time to record a mix of love songs or other sentimental songs on a blank tape. Wrap the tape as beautifully as you would any other wedding gift.

There are certain items that adapt to every occasion, and can fit within your budget. Chapter Eight's "Generic Gifts" were developed for this purpose. Here are a few as examples:

FOOD
Food gifts can be found already prepared, or you can make them from scratch—thereby presenting the gift of your time. Unlike some of the gifts of "your time" mentioned earlier, food gifts require some expense, but you can keep the gift within your budget. Since the value of homemade food gifts is proportionately much greater than store bought versions, you can really stretch your dollar in this category.

Whether you are a gourmet chef or not, there are numerous recipes which are easy to make that are successful food gifts. If you do have some talent in the kitchen, don't ignore food gifts. There is nothing quite as nice as receiving freshly baked or cooked food that you didn't have to make yourself.

Desserts are a natural. From homemade cookies to fresh fruit pies, melt-in-your-mouth fudge or delicious specialty cakes. Don't forget main dish gifts too. Your family may have a special recipe for roasts or stews. Present them in freezer-ready containers. Just remember that any food gift that saves the recipient time will be appreciated. If you want the gift to last more than one meal, consider homemade jams, mustards, spices, or dressings.

You can adjust the amount of money you spend depending on what you make. Some items can be made for pennies for

The Lists

each serving. For many, you can save more money if you make a large quantity of the food and split it up for more than one gift. Food can really stretch! Last Christmas, my 14-year old nephew had a dilemma. He had $60 to buy 30 gifts! (He wanted to give gifts to his entire family, including aunts, uncles and cousins). He decided to make homemade chocolate chip cookies. Each person received cookies packaged in a clear plastic bag with a bright red ribbon. His gifts were a success and he stayed within his budget! They were thoughtful, personally made and packaged, and they tasted good too!

If you're not sure what to make and your own cookbooks are not inspiring you, visit your local public library. Most libraries have lots of cookbooks, many of which are written solely about gifts that come from your kitchen.

For foods that you purchase as gifts, look for sales. Or, if you put together a package of food items, do it yourself. Many stores will make up the package for you—but for twice or three times the price. Instead, make the selection of individual items yourself and festively wrap them in a box, basket or container found around the house. Select a half dozen fancy spices, or smoked oysters, gourmet jams, cheese or wines. Or pick out less exotic foods like fresh fruits, favorite cookies or candies. Package whatever items and amount fit within your budget, but personalize!

You will, of course, want to weigh your time with your money. It may be in your interest to spend an extra dollar, rather than make an overly elaborate, time-consuming dish or food gift.

Or you might choose to spread the time and cost throughout the year. Example: A food gift idea that would be appropriate for a friend or relative who visits frequently is the offer to keep on hand a preferred food item. For example, Bob is a "Classic Coke" purist. His daughter gave him a wonderful personal gift by stating in a note that she would keep Classic Coke in her refrigerator just for him at all times. She must think of his needs whenever she shops for groceries. The cost is spread out throughout the year, so it's not a financial burden to her. And although the gift costs her money, the gift becomes of even greater value to Bob because it is also a gift of love and thoughtfulness. You can be sure he appreciates it!

BOOKS
You don't have to purchase the latest best sellers in hardback at their usual hefty price. Whether you want a baby shower gift for a girlfriend, birthday gift for your boss or a housegift thanking friends for a weekend of hospitality, you can turn to books every time! There are a number of discount bookstores as well as second-hand bookstores available so you often can present a package of books for under $10.

Baby shower:
Tie up 3 or 4 paperback books on baby care (include a funny one too!) with lots of ribbon and attach a baby rattle or similar toy.

Birthday gift for boss
Present a bestselling paperback book that he has expressed interest in, with three pieces of his favorite candy or chocolates.

Housegift
Either locate an impressive coffee table book on sale or put together a few paperbacks on a subject they have an interest in. If nothing immediately comes to mind, browse at the bookstore. There are always humorous books which, if given as a package, make a marvelous fun gift!

PHOTOS
For very little money you can present one or more photographs as a gift. Locate photos of your friend's first home or pet and present it in a frame. With a photo so personal, you don't need an expensive frame if you can't afford it. Just select a simple, classic design in wood or brass. Or make a frame by covering a cheap version with fabric or other attractive covering.

If you present more than one photo, make a montage in one large frame, or put them in a scrapbook. Since scrapbooks can be costly, instead locate a small "blank" book available at gift or office supply stores. The size of a regular book, they are often covered with fabric or colorful covers and

The Lists

include blank pages, so you can include your own writing. You may wish to add your own captions to the photos, or write in funny or inspirational quotes throughout.

For a large party where many people can chip in for gifts, splurge and get a nice big scrapbook. Then as the party proceeds, take instant photos of the attendees, paste them in the book and have each person write a personal note to the guest of honor by their picture. You might also have each participant bring along a photo taken earlier if they have one that would be appropriate to the event.

FRAMES
Even if you do not have a photograph, you can personalize the gift of a frame by inserting something inside the frame before you wrap it up in a gift box. You can write a sentimental or mushy note, or an inspirational quotation or poem. Or, clip out a cartoon, picture or headline from a newspaper or magazine.

Select the best frame you can afford. As mentioned above, you can find inexpensive frames and jazz them up with personal touches. But, for those gift recipients who collect exquisite possessions, a small quality frame is better to receive than a large frame of mediocre quality. Again, keep an eye out for sales throughout the year and occasionally poke around flea markets and antique shops for unique frames. Always keep a few frames on hand to present as the occasion pops up. They are particularly invaluable when you have an unexpected celebration and no time to find a gift! Won't you be the smart gift giver if, at the last minute, you present a $30 hand-etched bronze or marble frame—with a special note or insert, of course—that only cost you $7!

OFFICE ACCESSORIES
Office accessories come in all price ranges, so zero in on items you can afford. If you can't afford $40 bookends, get a $10 book. If you can't afford a $20 vase, present fresh flowers for $7. If you can't afford a $75 leather wastebasket, but it's exactly what your friend wants, chip in with friends.

Just stick within your budget. It's possible. One example of a low cost gift that could be given to almost anyone is a package of gold-plated paper clips (not real gold!) costing a few dollars. An established businessman would enjoy receiving them as well as a young person beginning a career, because they're of good quality and each time they used one they would think of you, their special friend.

STATIONERY
For less than $10, you can give pretty notecards, commemorative postage stamps, and a pen with ink that matches the stationery. If friends have just gotten married or moved, present them with stationery with their new name or address. You needn't get something elaborate, but get something they would enjoy using. Notice what kinds of stationery they use. For less expensive notes, visit office supply stores and see what kinds of note pads (for quick notes) can be personalized with the gift recipient's name.

SUBSCRIPTIONS
Most subscriptions to magazines or museums, or special interest clubs, are of reasonable cost. For example, a $5 membership to the AARP (American Association of Retired Persons) provides you with an annual subscription to their magazine, *Modern Maturity*. A slightly larger membership fee gets the incomparable *National Geographic* magazine. Or get *Reader's Digest* in Spanish for a friend who is fluent in the language. Present your friend with a magazine they would not splurge on for themselves, be it *People* or *Architectural Digest*. There are magazines for every interest and at many price levels.

* * * * *

Remember, too, to pick up gifts when you visit another city or a special exhibit (even in your home town). Note cards, playing cards or an ashtray (used as a soap dish), with a distinct scene or logo are economical and tell the person you were thinking of him or her.

Suggestions for inexpensive gifts include:

Socks	Serious or humorous socks
Flashlight	For any household. Consider a nightlight for baby gift.

The Lists

Flowers	Fresh cut or loose. Silk flowers are often a nice choice too. Present loose or in an arrangement.
Candles	One large decorative candle, or a box of 12 tapers.
Clock	A travel alarm, wristwatch or calculator with digital clock.
Costume jewelry	Look at second hand shops too.
Manicure, pedicure, facial, & massage	Get friends to chip in and give a day of luxury.
Kitchen gadgets	Something for everyone! Get two or three.
Scarf	Only if you know the person's colors and style.
Hat	From a baseball cap or bargain sun hat.
Pens	If you can't afford an expensive one, get a half dozen $1 pens or a box of No. 2 pencils with one's name imprinted.
Plants	All sizes.
T-shirt	With humorous saying or personal message.
Coffee mug	With a cartoon or saying that relates to the Giftee.
Map	It's practical and the person will appreciate it.
Jigsaw puzzle	Fine for a rainy day.

How to Stretch Your Dollar

No matter what the occasion, you can save money on gifts by remembering the following guidelines:

Split the Cost. Whether the gift costs $30 or $300. Example: If you determine that Susan and Joe would really like a TV for a wedding gift, don't despair. Get together with a bunch of their friends and have everyone contribute to the purchase. Whether it's a simple black-and-white or a fancy color TV, select the one within your budget(s).

GIFTING RIGHT

In addition to the jointly-purchased TV gift above, present a subscription to TV Guide or a case of popcorn or soda, or, to contrast the TV, you can present something small or impractical. Always "package" the gift with something that personalizes it even more, such as a handwritten note. For example, present their favorite bottle of wine, but write that it is for their "first weekend back home after the honeymoon." Or give a certificate for a home-delivered pizza and a coupon for a VCR rental. Your specific message suggesting how to use the gift shows your thoughtfulness and personalizes a material item.

Be on the look-out for sales. Purchase items at 50-75% off! Pick up a $75 crystal bowl (suitable for fruit, desserts, candies, even potato chips!) for $25. Or a $25 frame for $10. Or a $10 bottle of wine for $5. It goes on and on.

Rent, don't buy. If you can't afford to buy a VCR movie, present a coupon for the rental of 1, 2 or 3 movies. Include a box of ready-to-microwave popcorn. You can rent other items also. A group of friends could rent a limousine for the day. Or rent a canoe or bicycle. Rent a gown for a black tie event. Or provide the birthday boy or girl with a day at a health club or arrange to go horseback riding. If the item is impractical or too costly for you to buy, there may be a way to get use of that item or service temporarily.

Package the Gift Yourself. Another way to save money is to purchase items before they are packaged by the retailers. For example, rather than rely on a florist to make an arrangement (a modest flower arrangement can cost $30), pick out the flowers yourself and present them loose. For $7 you can present five impressive tall-stemmed flowers or a healthy bunch of smaller flowers. Most people have a vase or can fashion a container to hold the flowers.

Investments. There are many gifts that can cost an enormous amount, but not if spread out throughout the years. For example, make it an annual tradition to give a child, close friend or relative, a few shares in a mutual fund. Provide what you can afford each year. Even with a modest annual investment, the fund will continue to accumulate and be quite healthy in ten or twenty years. Savings bonds can also be presented as gifts. When presented over many years, these seemingly "cold" money gifts will become a treasured tradition.

Greeting cards. There are greeting cards for every occasion and just about any situation. Use them with gifts, or as a gift. People are delighted to be acknowledged, so don't underestimate the value of a single card, or a hand-written personal note on a special day.

Appreciation. Remember that it costs you nothing to say something nice to a person and remember them on a special day. We can all afford to give the gift of appreciation. And, if appropriate, throw in a hug!

TWELVE

A 1001 GIFT IDEAS — MASTERING YOUR GIFT SEARCH

The following pages list thousands of gift ideas. These are organized by the new categories you learned in the first section: the gift occasion, age group of the recipient and gift purpose.

Use this chapter as you would use your favorite restaurant guide. Let me explain. If you were to take friends or relatives out to dinner, you would want to select a "special" restaurant. You would want to choose a place with food and atmosphere that would please your friends the most. A common dilemma for many of us is that when it is time to come up with that perfect restaurant, we go blank. It's absurd, you know, because you know every restaurant in town. If you only had a few ideas to get your mind moving in the right direction. You want to see a few choices so you can select the best restaurant for the most memorable evening. So, what do you do when confronted with this situation? You get your restaurant guide which provides you with lots of ideas from which to choose.

That's what you want to do with gifts—match your friends' styles and desires with the most perfect gifts. This chapter will give you plenty of ideas.

As outlined throughout **Gifting Right**, the gift process and gift ideas can be broken down into categories. Here, too, the thousands of gift ideas are broken down by age, occasion and gift purpose, from only 200 generic and specific items. Naturally, you will find the gift-choosing process more manageable by looking at only 200 gift suggestions. Yet, as you use these lists, you will discover how each item can lead to more creative ideas, and almost every gift choice out there.

For example, a dozen of the 200 items are listed below with explanations of why they were listed in a certain category and how you might use the suggestion as a catalyst for other gift ideas.

You may or may not agree with some of these suggestions based on your own lifestyle and preferences. And that's okay. These gift ideas are elaborated upon to stimulate your imagination, because you are learning that successful gift giving is a creative process.

Examples of Gift Choices

Appliance, electric—It might seem odd at first to list youngsters as good recipients for electric appliances until one realizes that *children and teens* would enjoy receiving radios and clocks or new gadgets found at gift, toy or novelty shops. For adults, this category could include electric razors, microwave ovens, humidifiers or vaporizers/face steamers or electric toothbrushes. There are appliances for every one and every room.

Artist Supplies—From a box of crayons and a coloring book for kids, to contributing charcoal, brushes, to one's painting accessories, 10 pounds of clay for sculpting, or a box of 2,000 sheets of pin-feed computer paper for a writer.

Bar Accessories—Cork screws, decanters, a bottle of fine scotch, a serving tray lined with little bottles (bitters, tabasco, orange blossom water, Rose's lime juice, dry vermouth), a case of Perrier or seltzer water. Think of anything to use with a bar, by the bar, or near the bar.

Barbeque accessories—Barbeque accessories can be costly when buying more than one, so this is a fine category for *wedding showers* and *second weddings*. You might also consider presenting a larger grill instead, if the couple has been scrimping by with a $5 hibachi. With a higher quality grill, they can bake and smoke foods, too.

Barometer—A barometer should make your mind flow to other weather-measuring instruments — thermometers, rain measurers, humidifiers — or other electronic measuring gadgets, like a compass for a kid going to camp, or a car compass as a (practical) joke for a friend who is lousy with directions. Thermometers/barometers can be found mounted on wood plaques which are perfect for business executives' offices, or large-faced thermometers can be installed outside the kitchen window or back door so the whole family can check the forecast each day.

Cards, playing—A handy and attractive gift for *Adults* if you know they play card games like bridge, weekly or daily, and are always in need of new, clean cards. Even if friends do not play cards frequently, presenting a deck of cards engraved with their initials and color coordinated to the living room or other card-playing room creates a different and fun gift. The category should also lead your mind to other card or board games — from Monopoly and backgammon to dominoes.

Certificates—Certificates are listed because one can create a certificate for anyone or any occasion. (See Chapter Eight, Generic Gifts, for ways to select or create great certificates, and also Chapter Nine for a list of services that adapt well to certificates. Most items are adaptable if you "shape" them into the form of a service or product to be provided in the future or a gift where you allow the recipient to choose the style or colors.)

Gift certificate examples follow for every category:

Children
- "3 games of bowling for you and a friend, plus hot dogs and sodas" (time to be arranged).
- Offer to bring a friend's child and three friends to an amusement park.

Teenagers
- Certificate to local music shop "for cassette of your choice." (If you wanted to spend about $12-$15, you might make the amount out to $14 (their age) or $12.73 (if they were born in December, the 12th month, of 1973).

Acquiring Adults
- Babysitting provided for a weekend (so your friends can pamper themselves at home or away). As a friend,

you can either pay for a babysitter, or babysit their children at your house for the weekend, if you also have kids. Or have their kids over anyway, even if you don't have kids!

Adults with Everything
- Cooking lesson for Black Forest Cake, dim sum, or maki sushi.

Seniors
- "A car and driver to bring you to the city for shopping." (If you can't afford a limousine, be the driver yourself, which adds your company as part of the gift).

Acquaintances
- "Cocktails napkins engraved in the initials and colors of your choice."

Office Colleagues (Executive level)
- A round trip ticket to New York (or their hometown, or another city to visit friends or relatives).

Friends
- A money certificate that *contributes* to a pipe, coins, stamps, a volume of books or whatever items a person loves or collects. (If you don't know the cost of the item but assume it might be more expensive than you can afford, give the certificate that says "A contribution to..." For example, a box of cigars may be out of your price range, so presenting "A contribution to a box of XYZ cigars" would be fine. Or else, present only what you can afford, "5 Jamaican or Havana cigars." Of course, you could actually purchase the 5 cigars, but by providing a certificate you "add" to the gift because the person has the fun of going to the tobacco shop and enjoying the aroma of the surroundings. He may decide to try another brand and buy a few extra items on the trip. One must make sure, of course, that it would not be a burden for the person to go to the store. Also, it's better to *contribute* to the best quality

GIFTING RIGHT

than to *purchase* a lower quality version, if you're on a budget.

Anniversaries
- A dinner for two at their favorite or a highly popular restaurant.

Birthdays
- A one-year subscription to a magazine that the Giftees would not splurge on themselves.

Baby Shower
- "A comforting massage" for the mother-to-be, with a baby rattle attached to the certificate.

Get Well Present
- "10 individually selected pieces of Godiva chocolate" (or other gourmet chocolates, pastries or cookies available in your area).

New Home/Housewarming
- Certificate to interior decorator's services for advice.

Host/Hostess
- $5 ice cream certificate to local shop/parlor. (The amount might include enough for the whole family including children).

Office occasion
- Hire a limousine to take someone to and from a special event.

Wedding
- Choice of fireplace equipment.

Wedding Shower
- Certificate to custom-frame a favorite wedding or honeymoon photograph.

Second Wedding
- A lesson for two in golf, tennis or dancing the tango.

The Lists

Functional Gift
- Offer to develop 3 rolls of film from an upcoming trip.

Decorative Gift
- Choice of 20 candles.

Fun/Sentimental Gift
- 10 pounds of birdseed to fill birdhouse (include a store-bought or home-made birdhouse if you can).

Durable Gift
- $15 certificate for "silk flowers of your own choosing." Many department stores and some five-and-dime stores stock nylon flowers which look as good as silk, are easier to clean and are a fraction of the cost!

As you can see from the above, one can fashion "certificates" for any product or service, and for any occasion.

Clothes brush—Those concerned with appearance might be given three brushes — one for home, office, the car or travel. Consider getting these handsome people a nice mirror, too, for home or office.

Ethnic Cookware—Select whatever cuisine you think your friends would desire. For example, if you chose Chinese, you could present chopsticks and chopstick rests, decorative china bowls and spoons. Or collect food samples and present them in bamboo containers or on a bamboo tray.

Kites—Fun, playful toys, games for all ages.

Doormat—If the mat is embossed with the newlyweds name or initials or of a higher quality material, it's fine as a gift for a *wedding shower*.

Escargot utensils—Let this category challenge you to think about other "gourmet" utensils and serving pieces. Asparagus steamers, zucchini corers, lemon zesters. Soufflé or trifle dishes. Caviar or shrimp dishes. Demitasse spoons.

Exercise equipment—Gifts in this category are also great for *Seniors* to help them maintain their health and flexibility. There are many exercise aids that are designed for less strenuous activities and for those who are not exercise fanatics, but desire good health.

Herbs—Wonderful for *wedding* and *shower* gifts if you give a large quantity or include an attractive spice rack with the herbs and spices.

Ice cream scoop—Present the scoop with a gallon of ice cream or a coupon to an ice cream shop.

Microscope—Let this item remind you of scientific and educational projects, games or toys for *kids* or other hobbies for *adults*.

Organizers—See listed under Generic Gifts, Chapter Eight.

Photographs—Photos may not always be appreciated by *Children/Teenagers* as the sole gifts, so present them in a colorful frame or with the kid's own scrapbook or photo album. These "add-ons" would give photographs the zest needed to make them a great gift for kids.

Plants—Great for *second wedding* gifts, for couples who already have accumulated the basics. But not just any old small plant or two. Consider giving plants, trees or bushes that can be planted outside on their property (if they own a house) or beautiful indoor plants if they have an apartment or condo.

Safe—Giving a safe to a *Teenager* might give them a sense of maturity and fun having their little bit of privacy.

Slippers—Fun as *multiple* gifts. Present identical pairs for every family member. Kids might enjoy wearing grownup slippers like their parents; or every one would get great laughs

THE LISTS

if everyone was presented with silly slippers such as those of elephant, rabbit, or bear faces. As a *wedding shower* gift, get sexy Jean Harlow-type slippers for the bride, leather slippers for the groom. Slippers should also make you think of related bedroom or evening items like smoking jackets, foot stools, reading lamps, books, and other comforts, like champagne and caviar.

Sports Clothes—Can be presented to *Acquaintances*, but only if you know enough about their style and size. These items are okay as a gift for a wedding *Anniversary* gift, but only if you get a his & her set, because anniversaries honor a couple, not one individual. Clothes are good as *Get well* gifts, if sports-related items will make people feel better, because it will remind them they will be well soon.

Stuffed animal—Can be given as a *Host/Hostess* gift for dinner or a weekend thanks, for the children of the hosts, or if the stuffed creature (or toy) is related to a good-natured joke.

Sweaters—Like all clothes, sweaters are tricky to present if you don't know one's style or size. Unless you get the most classic styles, you should consider if the girl is more like Dolly Parton or Cher. And is the man's build an Arnold Schwarzenegger or Pee-Wee Herman-type? Does the youngster look like a child model or a Smurf? Stick to classic styles to be safe.

Thermos Decanter—Even *Teenagers* would enjoy a thermos at sports events or for camping. For *Adults*, present a thermos for commuting, sports events, or desk models for business executives.

Vase—It's not the best gift for *Seniors*, who generally have already accumulated enough decorative pieces. If it comes with flowers or plants as the main gift, then it's okay.

Wastebasket—Cheerful, colorful wastebaskets for *Teenagers* will brighten their bedrooms and direct them toward tidiness. High quality and expensive wastebaskets also can be an attractive accessory for any room, complementing the interior decoration. They are appropriate for every room in the house and are used by persons of all incomes, therefore, they are great gifts for *Acquiring Adults*, for the office or home.

The preceding descriptions will help you to be creative in using the following lists. As you become accustomed to the suggestions, you may want to write in your own ideas. *Gifting Right* **is your personal gift guide. Write in any gift ideas that will help you in the future.**

PRACTICAL GIFTS
For Children

Address book
Appliances, electric—lamp, radio, toys
Artist supplies
Beach items
Bicycle
Bird feeder
Bookends
Bookmarks
Books
Calculator
Calendars
Certificates
Child's dinnerware set
Clocks
Computer accessories—software
Desk accessories
Flashlight—for camping or bedroom
Food—one item, a basket of goodies, or an invitation out
Frames
Gloves
Hats
Jumprope
Key ring/holder
Knapsack
Knife, Swiss Army
Lamps
Lessons—contribute to
Metronome
Microscope
Organizers
Pajamas
Pens, pencils
Pet accessories
Radio
Robe
Seeds (flowers or food)
Shoe polish kits
Sleeping bag
Slippers
Sporting goods, clothes
Stationery
Stuffed animals
Subscriptions
Sweater
Tennis items
Wastebasket
Wristwatch

PRACTICAL GIFTS
For Teenagers

Address book
Appliances, electric
Artist supplies
Barometer
Beach items
Bicycle & accessories
Binoculars
Bird feeder
Bookends
Bookmarks

Books
Bookshelves
Calendars
Calculator
Certificates
Clocks
Computer accessories
Desk accessories
Exercise equipment
Flashlight
Food
Frames
Gloves
Hair appliances
Handbags
Hardware tools
Hats
Jumprope
Key ring/holder
Knapsack
Knife, Swiss Army
Lamps
Lessons—contribute to
Luggage
Metronome
Microscope
Mirrors
Organizers
Pajamas
Pens, pencils
Pet accessories
Photo album
Radio

Robe
Rug
Safe for valuables
Shoe polish kits
Sleeping bag
Slippers
Sporting goods, clothes
Sweater
Telephone
Tennis items
Thermos container
Towels—monogrammed
Wastebasket
Wristwatch

**PRACTICAL GIFTS
For Acquiring Adults**

Address book
Appliances, electric
Artist supplies
Attaché case
Auto accessories
Bar accessories
Barbeque accessories
Beach items
Bedspread stand
Blanket
Bookends
Bookmarks
Books
Bookshelves
Calculator
Calendars

The Lists

- Camera accessories
- Candle snuffer
- Candles
- Candlesticks
- Certificates
- Clocks
- Clothes
- Clothes brush
- Coffee maker
- Coffee mugs
- Coffee, teas
- Color charting
- Computer accessories
- Cookware
- Decanters
- Desk accessories
- Dining accessories
- Door knocker
- Doormat
- Earphones
- Escargot utensils
- Ethnic cuisine cookware
- Evening bag
- Exercise equipment
- Expresso pot
- Facial, pedicure, manicure
- Fire escape ladder
- Fire extinguisher
- Fireplace accessories
- Flashlight
- Flowers, silk
- Food
- Footstool
- Frames
- Furniture
- Glasses, drinking
- Gloves
- Hair appliances
- Hangers, wood
- Hardware tools
- Hats
- Herbs, spices
- Humidor
- Hurricane lamp
- Ice bucket
- Ice cream scoop
- Iron and board
- Jumprope
- Key rack
- Key ring/holder
- Kitchen accessories
- Kitchen appliances
- Kitchen gadgets
- Knapsack
- Knife, Swiss Army
- Knives, cheese
- Ladder
- Lamps
- Lessons—contribute to
- Letter opener
- Linens, bed
- Linens, table
- Liqueurs/Brandy
- Log carrier
- Luggage
- Microwave dishes

GIFTING RIGHT

Mirrors
Opera glasses
Organizers
Pajamas
Paperweight
Pens, pencils
Pet accessories
Photo album
Picnic basket
Plants
Radio
Robe/dressing gown
Rug
Sachéts
Salad bowl
Scarf
Shoe trees
Sleeping bag
Slippers
Sporting goods, clothes
Stationery
Subscriptions
Sweater
Teapot
Telephone
Tennis items
Thermos decanter
Time, yours
Toilet case
Towels
Towels, guest
Travel accessories
Vase

Wallet
Wastebasket
Wine coaster
Wine rack
Wristwatch

**PRACTICAL GIFTS
For Established Adults**

Address book
Appliances, electric
Artist supplies
Attaché case
Auto accessories
Bar accessories
Barbeque accessories
Barometer
Bed tray
Bedspread stand
Binoculars
Blanket
Bookends
Bookmarks
Books
Bookshelves
Brandy snifters
Calculator
Calendars
Camera accessories
Candle snuffer
Candles
Candlesticks
Certificates
Clocks

The Lists

- Clothes brush
- Coffee mugs
- Coffee, teas
- Color charting
- Computer accessories
- Cookware
- Decanters
- Decorative accessories
- Desk accessories
- Dining accessories
- Door knocker
- Doormat
- Escargot utensils
- Ethnic cuisine cookware
- Evening bag
- Exercise equipment
- Expresso pot
- Facial, pedicure, manicure
- Fire escape ladder
- Fire extinguisher
- Fireplace accessories
- Flashlight
- Flowers, silk
- Food
- Footstool
- Frames
- Glasses, drinking
- Gloves
- Hair accessories
- Hair appliances
- Handbags
- Hangers, wood
- Hats
- Home-made food
- Humidor
- Hurricane lamps
- Ice bucket
- Ice cream scoop
- Key rack
- Key ring/holder
- Kitchen accessories
- Kitchen appliances
- Kitchen gadgets
- Knives, cheese
- Ladder
- Lamps
- Lap desk
- Lessons—contribute to
- Letter opener
- Linens, bed
- Linens, table
- Log carrier
- Massage
- Metronome
- Microwave dishes
- Mirrors
- Mugs
- Napkin rings
- Opera glasses
- Organizers
- Pajamas
- Paperweight
- Pens, pencils
- Pet accessories
- Photo album
- Picnic basket

Gifting Right

- Plants
- Radio
- Remote control
- Robe/dressing gown
- Rug
- Sachêts
- Shoe trees
- Silver tarnish cloth
- Slippers
- Sporting goods, clothes
- Subscriptions
- Sweater
- Teapot
- Telephone
- Tennis items
- Thermos decanter
- Time, yours
- Towels, guest
- Travel accessories
- Vase
- Walking stick
- Wallet
- Wastebasket
- Wine coaster
- Wine rack
- Wristwatch

PRACTICAL GIFTS
For Seniors

- Address book
- Appliances, electric
- Artist supplies
- Auto accessories
- Barbeque accessories
- Barometer
- Beach items
- Bed tray
- Bedspread stand
- Binoculars
- Bird feeder
- Blanket
- Bookends
- Bookmarks
- Books
- Calculator
- Calendars
- Camera accessories
- Candles
- Certificates, personalized
- Clocks
- Coffee maker
- Coffee mugs
- Coffee, teas
- Computer accessories
- Desk accessories
- Door knocker
- Doormat
- Exercise equipment
- Facial, pedicure, manicure
- Fire escape ladder
- Fire extinguisher
- Fireplace accessories
- Flashlight
- Food
- Footstool
- Frames

The Lists

Glasses, drinking
Hair appliances
Hammock
Handbags, tote bags
Hats
Herbs, spices
Housewares
Humidors
Hurricane lamps
Key rack
Key ring/holder
Kitchen accessories
Kitchen appliances
Kitchen gadgets
Knife, Swiss Army
Knives, cheese/canape
Lamps
Lap desk
Lessons—contribute to
Letter opener
Log carrier
Massage
Metronome
Mugs
Napkin rings
Opera glasses
Organizers
Pajamas
Pens, pencils
Pet accessories
Photo album
Radio
Remote control

Robe/dressing own
Rug
Sachéts
Seeds (flower or food)
Sporting goods, clothes
Stationery
Step (kitchen) ladder
Subscriptions
Suspenders
Sweater
Teapot
Telephone
Tennis items
Time, yours
Towels, guest
Travel accessories
Walking stick
Wine coasters
Wristwatch

**PRACTICAL GIFTS
For Acquaintances**

Address book
Appliances, electric
Artist supplies
Auto accessories
Bar accessories
Barometer
Beach items
Bird feeder
Blanket
Bookends
Bookmarks

GIFTING RIGHT

- Books
- Brandy snifters
- Calculator
- Calendars
- Camera accessories
- Candle snuffer
- Candles
- Candlesticks
- Certificates, personalized
- Clocks
- Coffee maker
- Coffee mugs
- Coffee, teas
- Computer accessories
- Cookware
- Decanters
- Decorative accessories
- Desk accessories
- Dining accessories
- Door knocker
- Doormat
- Escargot utensils, or for other special dishes
- Ethnic cuisine cookware
- Expresso pot
- Fire escape ladder
- Fire extinguisher
- Fireplace accessories
- Food
- Frames
- Glasses, drinking
- Handbags, tote bags
- Hangers, wood
- Hardware tools
- Herbs, spices
- Housewares
- Hurricane lamps
- Ice bucket
- Key rack
- Key ring/holder
- Kitchen gadgets
- Knapsack
- Knife, Swiss Army
- Knives, cheese/canape
- Lamps
- Lap desk
- Lessons—contribute to
- Letter opener
- Linens, bed
- Linens, table
- Luggage
- Metronome
- Microwave dishes
- Mirrors
- Mugs
- Napkin rings
- Organizers
- Pens, pencils
- Pet accessories
- Photo album
- Radio
- Salad bowl
- Seeds (flower or food)
- Stationery
- Subscriptions
- Teapot

The Lists

Telephone
Tennis items
Thermos container
Time, yours
Towels
Towels, guest
Travel accessories
Vase
Wine coasters
Wine rack
Wristwatch

**PRACTICAL GIFTS
For Office Colleagues**

Address book
Appliances, electric
Artist supplies
Attaché case
Auto accessories
Bar accessories
Barometer
Binoculars
Bookends
Bookmarks
Books
Bookshelves
Brandy snifters
Calculator
Calendars
Camera accessories
Certificates, personalized
Clocks
Coffee mugs

Coffee, teas
Computer accessories
Decanters
Desk accessories
Expresso pot
Food
Frames
Furniture
Glasses, drinking
Hangers, wood
Humidors
Ice bucket
Key rack
Key ring/holder
Knife, Swiss Army
Lamps
Lap desk
Lessons—contribute to
Luggage
Mirrors
Mugs
Organizers
Pens, pencils
Radio
Rug
Stationery
Subscriptions
Teapot
Telephone
Tennis items
Thermos container
Time, yours
Towels, guest

Travel accessories
Vase
Wastebasket
Wristwatch

**PRACTICAL GIFTS
For Friends**

Address book
Appliances, electric
Artist supplies
Attaché case
Auto accessories
Bar accessories
Barbeque accessories
Beach items
Bed tray
Bedspread stand
Bird feeder
Blanket
Bookends
Bookmarks
Books
Bookshelves
Brandy snifters
Calculator
Calendars
Camera accessories
Candle snuffer
Candles
Candlesticks
Certificates, personalized
Clocks
Clothes brush

Coffee maker
Coffee mugs
Coffee, teas
Color charting
Computer accessories
Cookware
Decanters
Decorative accessories
Desk accessories
Dining accessories
Door knocker
Doormat
Escargot utensils, or for other special dishes
Ethnic cuisine cookware
Evening bag
Exercise equipment
Expresso pot
Facial, pedicure, manicure
Fire escape ladder
Fire extinguisher
Fireplace accessories
Flashlight
Food
Footstool
Frames
Furniture
Glasses, drinking
Hair appliances
Hammock
Handbags, tote bags
Hangers, wood
Hardware tools

The Lists

- Hats
- Herbs, spices
- Housewares
- Humidor
- Hurricane lamps
- Ice bucket
- Iron and board
- Jumprope
- Key rack
- Key ring/holder
- Kitchen accessories
- Kitchen appliances
- Kitchen gadgets
- Knapsack
- Knife, Swiss Army
- Knives, cheese/canape
- Lamps
- Lap desk
- Lessons—contribute to
- Letter opener
- Linens, bed
- Linens, table
- Log carrier
- Luggage
- Massage
- Metronome
- Microwave dishes
- Mirrors
- Mugs
- Napkin rings
- Opera glasses
- Organizers
- Pajamas
- Pens, pencils
- Pet accessories
- Photo album
- Picnic basket
- Radio
- Remote control
- Robe/dressing gown
- Rug
- Sachéts
- Safe for valuables
- Salad bowl
- Seeds (flower or food)
- Shoe polish kits
- Shoe trees
- Sleeping bag
- Slippers
- Sporting goods, clothes
- Stationery
- Subscriptions
- Suspenders
- Sweater
- Teapot
- Telephone
- Tennis items
- Thermos container
- Time, yours
- Toilet case (for travel)
- Tools
- Towels
- Towels, guest
- Travel accessories
- Vase
- Walking stick

Wastebasket
Wine coasters
Wine rack
Wristwatch

**PRACTICAL GIFTS
For Birthday/Annual**

Address book
Appliances, electric
Artist supplies
Attaché case
Auto accessories
Bar accessories
Barbeque accessories
Barometer
Beach items
Bed tray
Bedspread stand
Bicycle
Binoculars
Bird feeder
Blanket
Bookends
Bookmarks
Books
Bookshelves
Brandy snifters
Calculator
Calendars
Camera accessories
Candle snuffer
Candles
Candlesticks

Certificates, personalized
Clocks
Clothes brush
Coffee maker
Coffee mugs
Coffee, teas
Color charting
Computer accessories
Cookware
Decanters
Decorative accessories
Desk accessories
Dining accessories
Door knocker
Doormat
Escargot utensils, or for other special dishes
Ethnic cuisine cookware
Evening bag
Exercise equipment
Expresso pot
Facial, pedicure, manicure
Fire escape ladder
Fire extinguisher
Fireplace accessories
Flashlight
Food
Footstool
Frames
Furniture
Glasses, drinking
Hair appliances
Hammock

The Lists

- Handbags, tote bags
- Hangers, wood
- Hardware tools
- Hats
- Herbs, spices
- Housewares
- Humidor
- Hurricane lamps
- Ice bucket
- Iron and board
- Jumprope
- Key rack
- Key ring/holder
- Kitchen accessories
- Kitchen appliances
- Kitchen gadgets
- Knapsack
- Knife, Swiss Army
- Knives, cheese/canape
- Lamps
- Lap desk
- Lessons—contribute to
- Letter opener
- Linens, bed
- Linens, table
- Log carrier
- Luggage
- Massage
- Metronome
- Microwave dishes
- Mirrors
- Mugs
- Napkin rings
- Opera glasses
- Organizers
- Pajamas
- Pens, pencils
- Pet accessories
- Photo album
- Picnic basket
- Radio
- Remote control
- Robe/dressing gown
- Rug
- Sachéts
- Safe for valuables
- Salad bowl
- Seeds (flower or food)
- Shoe polish kits
- Shoe trees
- Sleeping bag
- Slippers
- Sporting goods, clothes
- Stationery
- Step (kitchen) ladder
- Subscriptions
- Suspenders
- Sweater
- Teapot
- Telephone
- Tennis items
- Thermos container
- Time, yours
- Toilet case (for travel)
- Tools
- Towels

GIFTING RIGHT

Towels, guest
Travel accessories
Vase
Walking stick
Wastebasket
Wine coasters
Wine rack
Wristwatch

PRACTICAL GIFTS
For Office

Address book
Appliances, electric
Attaché case
Auto accessories
Barometer
Binoculars
Bookends
Bookmarks
Books
Bookshelves
Calculator
Calendars
Camera accessories
Certificates, personalized
Clocks
Coffee mugs
Coffee, teas
Computer accessories
Desk accessories
Frames
Furniture
Glasses, drinking

Humidor
Lamps
Letter opener
Luggage
Mirrors
Organizers
Pens, pencils
Rug
Stationery
Telephone
Travel accessories
Vase
Wastebasket

PRACTICAL GIFTS
For Get Well

Appliances, electric
Artist supplies
Bed tray
Bird feeder
Bookends
Bookmarks
Books
Camera accessories
Certificates
Coffee mugs
Computer accessories
Desk accessories
Evening bag
Exercise equipment
Facial, pedicure, manicure
Food
Footstool

The Lists

Frames
Hair appliances
Hats
Jumprope
Kitchen gadgets
Lap desk
Lessons—contribute to
Linens, bed
Massage
Mugs
Opera glasses
Pajamas
Pens, pencils
Photo album
Radio
Remote control
Robe/dressing gown
Seeds (flowers or food)
Slippers
Sporting goods, clothes
Subscriptions
Sweater
Teapot
Tennis items
Time, yours
Travel accessories
Vase

**PRACTICAL GIFTS
For Host/Hostess**

Appliances, electric
Bar accessories
Barbeque accessories
Bookends
Bookmarks
Books
Calendars
Candle snuffer
Candles
Certificates, personalized
Coffee mugs
Coffee, teas
Dining accessories
Door knocker
Doormat
Escargot utensils, or for other special dishes
Ethnic cuisine cookware
Expresso pot
Fireplace accessories
Food
Frames
Herbs, spices
Housewares
Key rack
Kitchen gadgets
Knives, cheese/canape
Letter opener
Linens, table
Napkin rings
Pens, pencils
Pet accessories
Photo album
Sachéts
Seeds (flower or food)
Stationery

139

Teapot
Tools
Towels, guest
Travel accessories
Vase
Wine coasters

**PRACTICAL GIFTS
For Housewarming**

Address book
Appliances, electric
Bar accessories
Barbeque accessories
Barometer
Bed tray
Bedspread stand
Binoculars
Bird feeder
Blanket
Bookends
Bookshelves
Brandy snifters
Camera accessories
Candles
Certificates, personalized
Clocks
Coffee maker
Coffee, teas
Cookware
Decanters
Decorative accessories
Dining accessories
Door knocker

Doormat
Ethnic cuisine cookware
Expresso pot
Fire escape ladder
Fire extinguisher
Fireplace accessories
Flashlight
Food
Footstool
Frames
Furniture
Glasses, drinking
Hammock
Hangers, wood
Hardware tools
Hats
Herbs, spices
Housewares
Humidor
Hurricane lamps
Iron and board
Key rack
Key ring/holder
Kitchen accessories
Kitchen appliances
Kitchen gadgets
Lamps
Letter opener
Linens, bed
Linens, table
Log carrier
Microwave dishes
Mugs

The Lists

Napkin rings
Organizers
Photo album
Radio
Rug
Safe for valuables
Seeds (flower or food)
Sleeping bag
Stationery
Step (kitchen) ladder
Subscriptions
Teapot
Telephone
Time, yours
Tools
Towels
Towels, guest
Vase
Wastebasket
Wine rack

**PRACTICAL GIFTS
For Wedding Showers**

Address book
Appliances, electric
Bar accessories
Bed tray
Blanket
Bookends
Camera accessories
Candle snuffer
Candlesticks
Certificates, personalized
Clocks
Coffee maker
Cookware
Dining accessories
Door knocker
Doormat
Ethnic cuisine cookware
Fire escape ladder
Flashlight
Footstool
Frames
Glasses, drinking
Herbs, spices
Housewares
Hurricane lamps
Ice bucket
Key rack
Kitchen accessories
Kitchen appliances
Kitchen gadgets
Knives, cheese/canape
Lamps
Letter opener
Linens, bed
Linens, table
Log carrier
Luggage
Microwave dishes
Mirrors
Mugs
Napkin rings
Opera glasses
Organizers

GIFTING RIGHT

Pajamas
Photo album
Picnic basket
Radio
Robe/dressing gown
Salad bowl
Sweater
Teapot
Time, yours
Tools
Towels
Towels, guest
Travel accessories
Vase
Wastebasket
Wine coasters
Wine rack

PRACTICAL GIFTS
For Weddings

Appliances, electric
Barbeque accessories
Bedspread stand
Brandy snifters
Candlesticks
Certificates, personalized
Clocks
Coffee mugs
Cookware
Decanters
Decorative accessories
Dining accessories
Door knocker

Escargot utensils, or for other special dishes
Ethnic cuisine cookware
Frames
Furniture
Glasses, drinking
Housewares
Hurricane lamps
Ice bucket
Kitchen appliances
Knives, cheese/canape
Lamps
Linens, bed
Linens, table
Luggage
Microwave dishes
Mirrors
Napkin rings
Radio
Rug
Salad bowl
Teapot
Telephone
Towels
Vase
Wine rack

PRACTICAL GIFTS
For Second Weddings

Address book
Appliances, electric
Bar accessories
Barbeque accessories

The Lists

- Barometer
- Beach items
- Bed tray
- Bedspread stand
- Binoculars
- Bird feeder
- Bookends
- Bookshelves
- Brandy snifters
- Camera accessories
- Candle snuffer
- Candlesticks
- Certificates, personalized
- Clocks
- Coffee maker
- Coffee mugs
- Cookware
- Decanters
- Decorative accessories
- Dining accessories
- Door knocker
- Escargot utensils, or for other special dishes
- Ethnic cuisine cookware
- Exercise equipment
- Expresso pot
- Fire escape ladder
- Fireplace accessories
- Footstool
- Frames
- Glasses, drinking
- Hammock
- Hangers, wood
- Housewares
- Humidor
- Hurricane lamps
- Ice bucket
- Kitchen accessories
- Kitchen appliances
- Knives, cheese/canape
- Lamps
- Letter opener
- Linens, bed
- Linens, table
- Luggage
- Microwave dishes
- Mirror
- Napkin rings
- Opera glasses
- Photo album
- Picnic basket
- Radio
- Rug
- Safe for valuables
- Salad bowl
- Stationery
- Teapot
- Telephone
- Time, yours
- Tools
- Towels
- Towels, guest
- Travel accessories
- Vase
- Wastebasket
- Wine coasters

**PRACTICAL GIFTS
For Baby Showers**

Appliances, electric
Blanket
Bookends
Certificates, personalized
Frames
Lamps
Organizers
Pajamas
Photo album
Robe/dressing gown
Rug
Slippers
Sweater
Towels

**PRACTICAL GIFTS
For Anniversaries**

Address book
Appliances, electric
Bar accessories
Barbeque accessories
Barometer
Bed tray
Bedspread stand
Binoculars
Bird feeder
Blanket
Bookends
Books
Bookshelves
Brandy snifters
Calendars
Candle snuffer
Candles
Candlesticks
Certificates, personalized
Clocks
Coffee maker
Coffee mugs
Computer accessories
Cookware
Decanters
Decorative accessories
Dining accessories
Door knocker
Escargot utensils, or for other special dishes
Ethnic cuisine cookware
Evening bag
Exercise equipment
Expresso pot
Fireplace accessories
Footstool
Frames
Glasses, drinking
Hammock
Housewares
Humidor
Hurricane lamps
Ice bucket
Kitchen accessories
Kitchen appliances

The Lists

- Kitchen gadgets
- Knives, cheese/canape
- Lamps
- Letter opener
- Linens, bed
- Linens, table
- Log carrier
- Luggage
- Microwave dishes
- Mirrors
- Mugs
- Napkin rings
- Opera glasses
- Photo album
- Picnic basket
- Radio
- Robe/dressing gown
- Rug
- Salad bowl, wood or glass
- Sleeping bag
- Sporting goods, clothes
- Stationery
- Teapot
- Telephone
- Thermos container
- Time, yours
- Tools
- Towels
- Towels, guest
- Travel accessories
- Vase
- Wastebasket
- Wine coasters
- Wine rack

DECORATIVE GIFTS
For Children

Address book
Backgammon/board games
Beach items
Bookends
Certificates, personalized
Christmas/Holiday ornaments
Clocks
Frames
Globe
Gloves
Jewelry
Pajamas
Photographs
Picnic basket
Posters
Prints
Radio
Sporting goods, clothes
Sweater
Wristwatch

DECORATIVE GIFTS
For Teenagers

Address book
Backgammon/board games
Barometer
Beach items
Bedspread
Buttons, for blazer, sweaters
Bookends
Bookshelves
Certificates, personalized
Christmas/Holiday ornaments
Clocks
Frames
Globe
Gloves
Jewelry
Lamps
Mirrors
Needlepoint
Pajamas
Photographs
Posters
Prints
Radio
Rug
Sporting goods, clothes
Sweater
Telephone
Towels
Wastebasket
Wristwatch

DECORATIVE GIFTS
For Acquiring Adults

Address book
Beach items
Bedspread stand
Blanket
Bookends

146

The Lists

- Bookshelves
- Brandy snifters
- Calendars
- Camera accessories
- Candle snuffer
- Candles
- Candlesticks
- Certificates, personalized
- Clocks
- Coffee mugs
- Cookware
- Decanters
- Decorative accessories
- Desk accessories
- Dining accessories
- Door knocker
- Doormat
- Escargot utensils, or for other special dishes
- Ethnic cuisine cookware
- Evening bag
- Expresso pot
- Fireplace accessories
- Footstool
- Frames
- Furniture
- Glasses, drinking
- Hats
- Housewares
- Humidor
- Hurricane lamps
- Ice bucket
- Iron and board
- Jumprope
- Key rack
- Kitchen accessories
- Knives, cheese/canape
- Lamps
- Letter opener
- Linens, bed
- Linens, table
- Luggage
- Microwave dishes
- Mirrors
- Mugs
- Napkin rings
- Opera glasses
- Organizers
- Pajamas
- Radio
- Robe/dressing gown
- Rug
- Sachéts
- Salad bowl
- Seeds (flower or food)
- Slippers
- Stationery
- Suspenders
- Sweater
- Teapot
- Telephone
- Tennis items
- Time, yours
- Towels
- Towels, guest
- Travel accessories

GIFTING RIGHT

Vase
Wastebasket
Wine coasters
Wine rack
Wristwatch

**DECORATIVE GIFTS
For Established Adults**

Address book
Beach items
Bed tray
Bedspread stand
Bird feeder
Blanket
Bookends
Books
Bookshelves
Calendars
Candle snuffer
Candles
Candlesticks
Certificates, personalized
Clocks
Coffee mugs
Color charting
Cookware
Decanters
Decorative accessories
Desk accessories
Dining accessories
Door knocker
Escargot utensils, or for other special dishes

Ethnic cuisine cookware
Evening bag
Fireplace accessories
Food
Footstool
Frames
Furniture
Glasses, drinking
Hats
Humidor
Hurricane lamps
Ice bucket
Key rack
Kitchen accessories
Knives, cheese/canape
Lamps
Letter opener
Linens, bed
Linens, table
Luggage
Microwave dishes
Mirrors
Mugs
Napkin rings
Opera glasses
Organizers
Pajamas
Photo album
Picnic basket
Radio
Robe/dressing gown
Rug
Sachéts

THE LISTS

Salad bowl
Slippers
Sporting goods, clothes
Stationery
Subscriptions
Suspenders
Sweater
Teapot
Telephone
Tennis items
Time, yours
Towels
Towels, guest
Vase
Walking stick
Wastebasket
Wine coasters
Wine rack
Wristwatch

**DECORATIVE GIFTS
For Seniors**

Address book
Beach items
Bed tray
Bedspread stand
Bird feeder
Blanket
Bookends
Bookmarks
Calendars
Candles
Certificates, personalized
Clocks
Coffee mugs
Cookware
Decanters
Decorative accessories
Desk accessories
Dining accessories
Door knocker
Doormat
Ethnic cuisine cookware
Evening bag
Expresso pot
Facial, pedicure, manicure
Fireplace accessories
Food
Footstool
Frames
Furniture
Glasses, drinking
Hats
Humidor
Hurricane lamps
Kitchen accessories
Kitchen gadgets
Lamps
Linens, bed
Linens, table
Luggage
Microwave dishes
Mirrors
Mugs
Napkin rings
Opera glasses

GIFTING RIGHT

Pajamas
Radio
Robe/dressing gown
Rug
Sachéts
Salad bowl
Stationery
Suspenders
Sweater
Teapot
Telephone
Time, yours
Towels
Towels, guest
Vase
Walking stick
Wastebasket
Wristwatch

**DECORATIVE GIFTS
For Acquaintances**

Address book
Backgammon/board games
Barometer
Beach items
Bookends
Brandy snifters
Candle snuffer
Candles
Candlesticks
Certificates, personalized
Clocks
Coffee mugs

Cookware
Decanters
Decorative accessories
Desk accessories
Dining accessories
Door knocker
Escargot utensils, or for other special dishes
Fireplace accessories
Flowers, silk/real
Frames
Globe
Gloves
Hangers, wood
Housewares
Hurricane lamps
Ice bucket
Jewelry
Key rack
Knives, cheese/canape
Lamps
Letter opener
Linens, bed
Linens, table
Mirrors
Napkin rings
Needlepoint
Photographs
Plants
Posters
Prints
Radio
Scarf

The Lists

Sculpture
Teapot
Telephone
Towels
Towels, guest
Travel accessories
Vase
Wine coasters
Wine rack
Wristwatch

**DECORATIVE GIFTS
For Office Colleagues**

Address book
Barometer
Bookends
Bookshelves
Certificates, personalized
Clocks
Coffee mugs
Decanters
Desk accessories
Dining accessories
Flowers, real/silk
Frames
Furniture
Hangers, wood
Humidor
Ice bucket
Jewelry
Key rack
Lamps
Letter opener

Mirrors
Photographs
Plants
Posters
Prints
Radio
Rug
Sculpture
Telephone
Towels, guest
Travel accessories
Vase
Wastebasket
Wristwatch

**DECORATIVE GIFTS
For Friends/Relatives**

Address book
Backgammon/board games
Beach items
Bedspread stand
Bird feeder
Blanket
Blazer buttons
Bookends
Bookshelves
Brandy snifters
Candle snuffer
Candles
Candlesticks
Certificates, personalized
Chess set

GIFTING RIGHT

Christmas/Holiday ornaments
Clocks
Coffee mugs
Cookware
Decanters
Decorative accessories
Desk accessories
Dining accessories
Door knocker
Escargot utensils, or for other special dishes
Evening bag
Fireplace accessories
Flowers, silk/real
Footstool
Frames
Furniture
Globe
Gloves
Hangers, wood
Housewares
Humidor
Hurricane lamps
Ice bucket
Jewelry
Key rack
Kitchen accessories
Knives, cheese/canape
Lamps
Letter opener
Linens, bed
Linens, table
Mirrors
Napkin rings
Nativity sets
Needlepoint
Pajamas
Photographs
Plants
Posters
Prints
Radio
Rug
Scarf
Sculpture
Sporting goods, clothes
Sweater
Teapot
Telephone
Towels
Towels, guest
Travel accessories
Vase
Walking stick
Wastebasket
Wine coasters
Wine rack
Wristwatch

DECORATIVE GIFTS
For Birthday/Annual

Address book
Backgammon/board games
Barometer
Beach items
Bedspread stand

The Lists

Blanket
Blazer buttons
Bookends
Books
Bookshelves
Brandy snifters
Candle snuffer
Candles
Candlesticks
Certificates
Chess set
Clock
Coffee mugs
Cookware
Decanters
Decorative accessories
Dining accessories
Door knocker
Evening bag
Fireplace accessories
Flowers, silk/real
Footstool
Frames
Furniture
Glasses, drinking
Globe
Gloves
Hair accessories
Humidors
Jewelry
Key rack
Kitchen accessories
Knives, cheese
Lamps
Letter opener
Linens, bed
Linens, table
Mirrors
Napkin rings
Needlepoint
Organizers
Pajamas
Paperweight
Plants
Posters
Prints
Radio
Rug
Salad bowl
Scarf
Sculpture
Seeds
Teapot
Telephone
Thermos decanter
Towels, guest
Travel accessories
Vase
Walking stick
Wastebasket
Wine coaster
Wine rack

**DECORATIVE GIFTS
For Office Occasions**

Address book

GIFTING RIGHT

Barometer
Bookends
Books
Bookshelves
Certificates, personalized
Clock
Frames
Furniture
Glasses, drinking
Humidor
Jewelry
Lamp
Letter opener
Photographs
Prints
Rug
Sculpture
Telephone
Travel accessories
Vase
Wastebasket

**DECORATIVE GIFTS
For Get Well**

Backgammon/board games
Certificates, personalized
Christmas/Holiday ornaments
Coffee mug
Evening bag
Flowers, silk/real
Footstool
Frames

Hair accessories
Jewelry
Linens, bed
Needlepoint
Pajamas
Photographs
Plants
Posters
Radio
Robe/dressing gown
Scarf
Sculpture
Sporting goods, clothes
Sweater
Teapot
Travel accessories
Vase

**DECORATIVE GIFTS
For Host/Hostess**

Backgammon/board games
Bookends
Candle snuffer
Candles
Certificates, personalized
Christmas/Holiday ornaments
Coffee mugs
Dining accessories
Door knocker
Escargot utensils, tools for other gourmet dishes
Fireplace accessories

The Lists

Flowers, silk/real
Frames
Housewares
Jewelry
Key rack
Kitchen accessories
Knives, cheese/canape
Letter opener
Linens, table
Napkin rings
Photographs
Plants
Posters
Prints
Scarf
Teapot
Towels, guest
Travel accessories
Vase
Wine coaster

**DECORATIVE GIFTS
For Housewarming**

Address book
Backgammon/board games
Barometer
Bedspread stand
Blanket
Bookends
Bookshelves
Brandy snifters
Candles
Certificates, personalized

Chess set
Clocks
Coffee mugs
Cookware
Decanters
Decorative accessories
Dining accessories
Door knocker
Fireplace accessories
Flowers, silk/real
Footstool
Frames
Furniture
Globe
Hangers, wood
Housewares
Humidors
Hurricane lamps
Key rack
Kitchen accessories
Lamps
Letter opener
Linens, bed
Linens, table
Mirrors
Napkin rings
Nativity sets
Photographs
Plants
Posters
Prints
Radio
Rug

Gifting Right

Sculpture
Teapot
Telephone
Towels
Towels, guest
Vase
Wastebasket
Wine rack

DECORATIVE GIFTS
For Wedding Shower

Address book
Blanket
Bookends
Candle snuffer
Candlesticks
Certificates, personalized
Chess set
Christmas/Holiday ornaments
Clocks
Coffee mugs
Cookware
Dining accessories
Door knocker
Escargot utensils, tools for other gourmet dishes
Flowers, silk/real
Footstool
Frames
Housewares
Hurricane lamps
Ice bucket

Key rack
Kitchen accessories
Knives, cheese/canape
Lamps
Letter opener
Linens, bed
Linens, table
Mirrors
Napkin rings
Nativity sets
Pajamas
Photographs
Prints
Radio
Sweater
Teapot
Towels
Towels, guest
Travel accessories
Vase
Wastebasket
Wine coaster
Wine rack

DECORATIVE GIFTS
For Weddings

Bedspread, or stand
Brandy snifters
Candlesticks
Certificates, personalized
Chess set
Clocks
Coffee mugs

The Lists

Cookware
Decanters
Decorative accessories
Dining accessories
Door knocker
Escargot utensils, or for other gourmet dishes
Fireplace accessories
Frames
Furniture
Housewares
Hurricane lamps
Ice bucket
Jewelry
Knives, cheese/canape
Lamps
Linens, bed
Linens, table
Mirrors
Napkin rings
Photographs
Radio
Rug
Sculpture
Teapot
Telephone
Towels
Vase
Wine rack

**DECORATIVE GIFTS
For Second Weddings**

Address book

Backgammon/board games
Barometer
Beach items
Bedspread stand
Blanket
Bookends
Bookshelves
Brandy snifters
Candle snuffer
Candlesticks
Certificates, personalized
Chess set
Christmas/Holiday ornaments
Clocks
Coffee mugs
Cookware
Decanters
Decorative accessories
Dining accessories
Door knocker
Escargot utensils, or other gourmet dishes
Fireplace accessories
Flowers, silk/real
Footstool
Frames
Globe
Hangers, wood
Housewares
Humidors
Hurricane lamps
Ice bucket
Jewelry

GIFTING RIGHT

Kitchen accessories
Knives, cheese/canape
Lamps
Letter opener
Linens, bed
Linens, table
Mirrors
Napkin rings
Nativity sets
Needlepoint
Photographs
Plants
Prints
Radio
Rug
Sculpture
Teapot
Telephone
Towels
Towels, guest
Travel accessories
Vase
Wastebasket
Wine coaster
Wine rack

**DECORATIVE GIFTS
For Baby Shower**

Blanket
Bookends
Certificates, personalized
Christmas/Holiday ornaments

Frames
Lamps
Pajamas
Posters
Prints
Rug
Sculpture
Sweater
Towels

**DECORATIVE GIFTS
For Anniversaries**

Address book
Backgammon/board game
Barometer
Bedspread stand
Blanket
Bookends
Bookshelves
Brandy snifters
Candle snuffer
Candles
Candlesticks
Certificates
Chess set
Clocks
Cookware
Decanters
Decorative accessories
Dining accessories
Door knocker
Fireplace accessories
Flowers, silk/real

The Lists

- Footstool
- Frames
- Globe
- Greeting card
- Jewelry
- Kitchen accessories
- Knives, cheese
- Lamps
- Letter opener
- Linens, bed
- Linens, table
- Mirrors
- Napkin rings
- Paperweight
- Plants
- Prints
- Radio
- Rug
- Salad bowl
- Sculpture
- Teapot
- Telephone
- Towels, guest
- Travel accessories
- Vase
- Wastebasket
- Wine coaster
- Wine rack

DURABLE GIFTS
For Children

Address book
Appliances, electric
Books
Certificates, personalized
Christmas/Holiday decorations
Clocks
Frames
Furniture
Globe
Jewelry
Metronome
Prints
Radio
Sleeping bag

DURABLE GIFTS
For Teenagers

Address book
Appliances, electric
Books
Certificates, personalized
Christmas/Holiday decorations
Clocks
Frames
Globe
Hardware tools
Housewares
Jewelry
Lamps
Luggage
Metronome
Mirrors
Needlepoint
Photo album
Prints
Radio
Rug
Sleeping bag

DURABLE GIFTS
For Acquiring Adults

Address book
Appliances, electric
Attaché case
Auto accessories
Bedspread stand
Books
Brandy snifters
Camera accessories
Candlesticks
Chess set
Christmas ornaments
Clocks
Clothes brush
Coffee maker
Coffee mugs
Cookware
Decanters
Decorative accessories
Dining accessories
Door knocker

The Lists

Escargot utensils
Ethnic cuisine cookware
Exercise equipment
Fire escape ladder
Fireplace accessories
Frames
Furniture
Glasses, drinking
Globe
Hammock
Hangers, wood
Hardware tools
Humidors
Hurricane lamps
Ice cream scoop
Iron and board
Jewelry
Kitchen accessories
Kitchen appliances
Kitchen gadgets
Knife, Swiss Army
Knives, cheese
Ladder
Lamps
Letter opener
Luggage
Magnets
Metronome
Microscope
Microwave dishes
Mirrors
Napkin rings
Nativity set

Opera glasses
Organizers
Paperweight
Photo album
Photographs
Plants
Prints
Radio
Rug
Safe for valuables
Salad bowl
Sculpture
Sleeping bag
Sporting goods, clothes
Stuffed animals
Subscriptions
Suspenders
Sweater
Teapot
Telephone
Thermos decanter
Toilet case
Travel accessories
Vase
Videocassettes
Wastebasket
Wine rack
Wristwatch

**DURABLE GIFTS
For Established Adults**

Address book
Appliances, electric

GIFTING RIGHT

Attaché case
Auto accessories
Barbeque accessories
Bedspread stand
Books
Brandy snifters
Camera accessories
Candlesticks
Certificates, personalized
Chess set
Christmas/Holiday decorations
Clocks
Coffee maker
Cookware
Decanters
Decorative accessories
Dining accessories
Door knocker
Escargot utensils, or for other gourmet dishes
Ethnic cuisine cookware
Fireplace accessories
Footstool
Frames
Glasses, drinking
Hardware tools
Housewares
Humidors
Hurricane lamps
Jewelry
Kitchen accessories
Kitchen appliances
Kitchen gadgets

Knives, cheese/canape
Lamps
Letter opener
Luggage
Metronome
Microwave dishes
Mirrors
Napkin rings
Opera glasses
Photo album
Prints
Radio
Rug
Sculpture
Sleeping bag
Teapot
Tools
Travel accessories
Vase
Wine rack

DURABLE GIFTS
For Seniors

Address book
Appliances, electric
Auto accessories
Barbeque accessories
Bedspread stand
Books
Camera accessories
Certificates, personalized
Clocks
Coffee maker

The Lists

Door knocker
Fireplace accessories
Footstool
Frames
Glasses, drinking
Housewares
Humidors
Hurricane lamps
Jewelry
Kitchen accessories
Kitchen appliances
Kitchen gadgets
Knives, cheese/canape
Lamps
Letter opener
Metronome
Napkin rings
Needlepoint
Opera glasses
Photo album
Prints
Radio
Rug
Sculpture
Teapot
Travel accessories

**DURABLE GIFTS
For Acquaintances**

Address book
Appliances, electric
Auto accessories
Books

Brandy snifters
Camera accessories
Candlesticks
Certificates, personalized
Clocks
Coffee maker
Cookware
Decanters
Decorative accessories
Dining accessories
Door knocker
Escargot utensils, or for other gourmet dishes
Ethnic cuisine cookware
Fireplace accessories
Frames
Globe
Hardware tools
Housewares
Hurricane lamps
Jewelry
Kitchen gadgets
Knives, cheese/canape
Lamps
Letter opener
Luggage
Metronome
Microwave dishes
Mirrors
Napkin rings
Needlepoint
Photo album
Prints

Gifting Right

Radio
Rug
Sculpture
Sleeping bag
Teapot
Tools
Travel accessories
Vase
Wine rack

**DURABLE GIFTS
For Office Colleagues**

Address book
Appliances, electric
Attaché case
Auto accessories
Books
Camera accessories
Certificates, personalized
Clocks
Coffee maker
Decanters
Decorative accessories
Frames
Furniture
Globe
Humidors
Jewelry
Lamps
Letter opener
Luggage
Mirrors
Prints

Radio
Rug
Sculpture
Travel accessories
Vase

**DURABLE GIFTS
For Friends/Relatives**

Address book
Appliances, electric
Attaché case
Auto accessories
Barbeque accessories
Bedspread stand
Books
Brandy snifters
Camera accessories
Candlesticks
Certificates, personalized
Chess set
Christmas/Holiday decorations
Clocks
Coffee maker
Cookware
Decanters
Decorative accessories
Dining accessories
Door knocker
Escargot utensils, or for other gourmet dishes
Ethnic cuisine cookware
Fireplace accessories

The Lists

Footstool
Frames
Furniture
Glasses, drinking
Globe
Hardware tools
Housewares
Humidors
Hurricane lamps
Jewelry
Kitchen accessories
Kitchen appliances
Kitchen gadgets
Knives, cheese/canape
Lamps
Letter opener
Luggage
Metronome
Microwave dishes
Mirrors
Napkin rings
Needlepoint
Opera glasses
Photo album
Prints
Radio
Rug
Sculpture
Sleeping bag
Teapot
Tools
Travel accessories
Vase

Wine rack

DURABLE GIFTS
For Birthday Gifts

Address book
Appliances, electric
Attaché case
Auto accessories
Barbeque accessories
Bedspread stand
Books
Brandy snifters
Camera accessories
Candlesticks
Certificates, personalized
Chess set
Christmas/Holiday decorations
Clocks
Coffee maker
Cookware
Decanters
Decorative accessories
Dining accessories
Door knocker
Escargot utensils, or for other gourmet dishes
Ethnic cuisine cookware
Fireplace accessories
Footstool
Frames
Furniture
Glasses, drinking

GIFTING RIGHT

Globe
Hardware tools
Housewares
Humidors
Hurricane lamps
Jewelry
Kitchen accessories
Kitchen appliances
Kitchen gadgets
Knives, cheese/canape
Lamps
Letter opener
Luggage
Metronome
Microwave dishes
Mirrors
Napkin rings
Needlepoint
Opera glasses
Photo album
Prints
Radio
Rug
Sculpture
Sleeping bag
Teapot
Tools
Travel accessories
Vase
Wine rack

DURABLE GIFTS
For Office Gifts

Address book
Appliances, electric
Attaché case
Auto accessories
Camera accessories
Certificates, personalized
Clocks
Frames
Furniture
Globe
Humidors
Lamps
Letter opener
Luggage
Mirrors
Prints
Radio
Rug
Sculpture
Travel accessories
Vase

DURABLE GIFTS
For Get Well Gifts

Appliances, electric
Books
Camera accessories
Certificates, personalized
Christmas/Holiday decorations

THE LISTS

Footstool
Frames
Jewelry
Kitchen gadgets
Needlepoint
Opera glasses
Photo album
Prints
Radio
Sculpture
Teapot
Travel accessories
Vase

**DURABLE GIFTS
For Host/Hostess Gifts**

Appliances, electric
Barbeque accessories
Books
Certificates, personalized
Christmas/Holiday decorations
Dining accessories
Door knocker
Escargot utensils, or for other gourmet dishes
Ethnic cuisine cookware
Fireplace accessories
Frames
Housewares
Jewelry
Kitchen accessories
Kitchen gadgets

Knives, cheese/canape
Letter opener
Napkin rings
Photo album
Prints
Teapot
Tools
Travel accessories
Vase

**DURABLE GIFTS
For Housewarming Gifts**

Address book
Appliances, electric
Barbeque accessories
Bedspread stand
Camera accessories
Certificates, personalized
Chess set
Clocks
Coffee maker
Cookware
Decanters
Decorative accessories
Dining accessories
Door knocker
Ethnic cuisine cookware
Fireplace accessories
Footstool
Frames
Furniture
Glasses, drinking
Globe

Hardware tools
Housewares
Humidors
Hurricane lamps
Kitchen accessories
Kitchen appliances
Kitchen gadgets
Lamps
Letter opener
Microwave dishes
Mirrors
Napkin rings
Photo album
Prints
Radio
Rug
Sculpture
Sleeping bag
Teapot
Tools
Vase
Wine rack

**DURABLE GIFTS
For Wedding Shower Gifts**

Address book
Appliances, electric
Camera accessories
Candlesticks
Certificates, personalized
Chess set
Christmas/Holiday decorations
Clocks
Coffee maker
Cookware
Dining accessories
Door knocker
Escargot utensils, or for other gourmet dishes
Ethnic cuisine cookware
Footstool
Frames
Housewares
Hurricane lamps
Jewelry
Kitchen accessories
Kitchen appliances
Kitchen gadgets
Knives, cheese/canape
Lamps
Letter opener
Luggage
Microwave dishes
Mirrors
Napkin rings
Opera glasses
Photo album
Prints
Radio
Teapot
Tools
Travel accessories
Vase
Wine rack

The Lists

DURABLE GIFTS
For Wedding Gifts

Appliances, electric
Barbeque accessories
Bedspread stand
Brandy snifters
Candlesticks
Certificates, personalized
Chess set
Clocks
Cookware
Decanters
Decorative accessories
Dining accessories
Door knocker
Escargot utensils, or for other gourmet dishes
Ethnic cuisine cookware
Frames
Furniture
Housewares
Hurricane lamps
Jewelry
Kitchen appliances
Knives, cheese/canape
Lamps
Luggage
Microwave dishes
Mirrors
Napkin rings
Prints
Radio
Rug
Sculpture
Teapot
Vase
Wine rack

DURABLE GIFTS
For Second Wedding Gifts

Address book
Appliances, electric
Barbeque accessories
Bedspread stand
Brandy snifters
Camera accessories
Candlesticks
Certificates, personalized
Chess set
Christmas/Holiday decorations
Clocks
Coffee maker
Cookware
Decanters
Decorative accessories
Dining accessories
Door knocker
Escargot utensils, or for other gourmet dishes
Ethnic cuisine cookware
Fireplace accessories
Footstool
Frames
Globe

Housewares
Humidors
Hurricane lamps
Jewelry
Kitchen accessories
Kitchen appliances
Knives, cheese/canape
Lamps
Letter opener
Luggage
Microwave dishes
Mirrors
Napkin rings
Needlepoint
Opera glasses
Photo album
Prints
Radio
Rug
Sculpture
Teapot
Tools
Travel accessories
Vase
Wine rack

**DURABLE GIFTS
For Baby Shower Gifts**

Appliances, electric
Certificates, personalized
Christmas/Holiday decorations
Frames

Lamps
Photo album
Prints
Rug
Sculpture

**DURABLE GIFTS
For Anniversary Gifts**

Address book
Appliances, electric
Barbeque accessories
Bedspread stand
Books
Brandy snifters
Candlesticks
Certificates, personalized
Chess set
Christmas/Holiday decorations
Clocks
Coffee maker
Cookware
Decanters
Decorative accessories
Dining accessories
Door knocker
Escargot utensils, or for other gourmet dishes
Ethnic cuisine cookware
Fireplace accessories
Footstool
Frames
Glasses, drinking

The Lists

Globe
Housewares
Humidors
Hurricane lamps
Jewelry
Kitchen accessories
Kitchen appliances
Kitchen gadgets
Knives, cheese/canape
Lamps
Letter opener
Luggage
Microwave dishes
Mirrors

Napkin rings
Needlepoint
Opera glasses
Photo album
Prints
Radio
Rug
Sculpture
Sleeping bag
Teapot
Tools
Travel accessories
Vase
Wine rack

Gifting Right

An emotional gift is determined by the relationship between you and the Giftee, so it can conceivably include anything. For these lists — which are merely an exercise in teaching you how to view gift choices with a new eye — I have listed only "fun" emotional items.

**EMOTIONAL/FUN GIFTS
For Children**

Appliances, electric
Artist supplies
Backgammon/board games
Balloons
Beach items
Belts
Bicycle
Bird feeder
Bookends
Bookmarks
Books
Bubblebath
Calculator
Calendars
Candy
Clothes
Computer accessories
Desk accessories
Flashlight
Food
Frames
Globe
Hair accessories
Hats
Jewelry
Jumprope
Key ring/holder
Knapsack
Lamps
Lessons—contribute to
Metronome
Mobiles
Models—cars, airplanes
Pajamas
Phonograph records
Posters
Prints
Puzzles
Radio
Robe/dressing gown
Shoe polish kits
Sleeping bag
Stationery
T-shirt
Tennis items
Toys
Yoyo

**EMOTIONAL/FUN GIFTS
For Teenagers**

Address book
Appliances, electric
Backgammon/board games

THE LISTS

Balloons
Barometer
Beach items
Belts
Bicycle
Binoculars
Bird feeder
Blazer buttons
Bookends
Bookmarks
Books
Bubblebath
Calculator
Calendars
Candy
Clothes
Computer accessories
Desk accessories
Flashlight
Food
Frames
Globe
Hair accessories
Hair appliances
Handbags
Hats
Jewelry
Jumprope
Key ring/holder
Knapsack
Lamps
Lessons—contribute to
Metronome

Mirrors
Mistletoe
Mobiles
Models—cars, airplanes
Movies
Museum membership
Needlepoint
Pajamas
Phonograph records
Posters
Prints
Puzzles
Radio
Robe/dressing gown
Shoe polish kits
Sleeping bag
Stationery
T-shirt
Tennis items
Yoyo

EMOTIONAL/FUN GIFTS
For Acquiring Adults

Appliances, electric
Artist supplies
Backgammon/board games
Balloons
Bar accessories
Beach items
Belts
Bicycle
Bird feeder
Blazer buttons

GIFTING RIGHT

- Bookends
- Bookmarks
- Books
- Brandy snifters
- Bubblebath
- Calculator
- Calendars
- Candy
- Clothes
- Cocktail napkins
- Coffee, teas
- Color charting
- Computer accessories
- Decanters
- Decorative accessories
- Desk accessories
- Dining accessories
- Door knocker
- Earphones
- Evening bag
- Expresso pot
- Fireplace accessories
- Flashlight
- Food
- Frames
- Globe
- Hair accessories
- Hair appliances
- Handbags
- Hats
- Humidors
- Hurricane lamps
- Jewelry
- Jumprope
- Key rack
- Key ring/holder
- Kitchen accessories
- Kitchen appliances
- Kitchen gadgets
- Knapsack
- Lamps
- Lessons—contribute to
- Letter opener
- Lingerie
- Liqueurs/Brandy
- Metronome
- Mirrors
- Mistletoe
- Movies
- Mugs
- Museum membership
- Napkin rings
- Nutcracker
- Nuts, canned
- Opera glasses
- Pajamas
- Phonograph records
- Photo album
- Picnic basket
- Posters
- Prints
- Puzzles
- Radio
- Robe/dressing gown
- Rug
- Sachéts

The Lists

Scarf
Sculpture
Sleeping bag
Smoking
Stationery
T-shirt
Teapot
Tennis items
Theater tickets
Time, yours
Towels, guest
Toys
Travel accessories
Wine
Wine coaster
Yoyo

EMOTIONAL/FUN GIFTS
For Established Adults

Artist supplies
Attaché case
Backgammon/board games
Balloons
Bar accessories
Barometer
Beach items
Bed tray
Binoculars
Bird feeder
Blazer buttons
Bookends
Bookmarks
Books
Brandy snifters
Bubblebath
Calculator
Calendars
Camera accessories
Candle snuffer
Candy
Clothes
Cocktail napkins
Coffee, teas
Color charting
Computer accessories
Decanters
Decorative accessories
Desk accessories
Dining accessories
Door knocker
Earphones
Evening bag
Expresso pot
Fireplace accessories
Flashlight
Food
Frames
Hair accessories
Hair appliances
Handbags
Hats
Humidors
Hurricane lamps
Jewelry
Key rack
Key ring/holder

Kitchen accessories
Kitchen appliances
Kitchen gadgets
Lamps
Lessons—contribute to
Letter opener
Lingerie
Liqueurs/Brandy
Metronome
Mirrors
Mistletoe
Movies
Mugs
Museum membership
Napkin rings
Nutcracker
Nuts, canned
Opera glasses
Pajamas
Phonograph records
Photo album
Picnic basket
Prints
Puzzles
Radio
Remote control
Robe/dressing gown
Rug
Sachéts
Scarf
Sculpture
Smoking accessories
T-shirt

Teapot
Tennis items
Theater tickets
Time, yours
Towels, guest
Toys
Travel accessories
Wine
Wine coaster
Yoyo

EMOTIONAL/FUN GIFTS
For Seniors

Appliances, electric
Artist supplies
Backgammon/board games
Balloons
Bar accessories
Barometer
Beach items
Bed tray
Binoculars
Bird feeder
Bookends
Bookmarks
Books
Calculator
Calendar
Camera accessories
Candy

THE LISTS

EMOTIONAL/FUN GIFTS
For Acquaintances

Appliances, electric
Artist supplies
Backgammon/board games
Bar accessories
Barometer
Beach items
Belts
Bird feeder
Bookends
Bookmarks
Books
Brandy snifters
Calculator
Calendars
Camera accessories
Candle snuffer
Candy
Certificates
Chocolates
Christmas ornaments
Clocks
Clocks
Clothes
Cocktail napkins
Coffee mugs
Coffee, teas
Computer accessories
Decanters
Decorative accessories
Desk accessories
Dining accessories
Escargot utensils
Expresso pot
Fireplace accessories
Flowers, silk/real
Food
Frames
Globe
Hair accessories
Handbags
Herbs, spices
Home-made food
Ice cream scoop
Jewelry
Key rack
Key ring/holder
Kitchen gadgets
Knapsack
Lamps
Lessons—contribute to
Letter opener
Liqueurs/Brandy
Metronome
Mirrors
Mistletoe
Mobiles
Models—cars, airplanes
Movies
Mugs
Museum membership
Napkin rings
Needlepoint
Nutcracker

Nuts, canned
Organizers
Paperweight
Pens, pencils
Perfume
Pet accessories
Phonograph records
Photo album
Plants
Posters
Prints
Puzzles
Radio
Scarf
Sculpture
Sleeping bag
Smoking accessories
Stationery
T-shirt
Teapot
Tennis items
Theater tickets
Time, yours
Towels, guest
Toys
Travel accessories
Wine
Wine coaster

**EMOTIONAL/FUN GIFTS
For Office Colleagues**

Appliances, electric
Artist supplies

Balloons
Bar accessories
Barometer
Binoculars
Bookends
Bookmarks
Books
Calculator
Calendars
Camera accessories
Candy
Certificates
Chocolate
Christmas ornaments
Clocks
Cocktail napkins
Coffee mugs
Coffee, teas
Computer accessories
Decanters
Desk accessories
Dining accessories
Expresso pot
Flowers, real/silk
Food
Frames
Home-made food
Jewelry
Key rack
Key ring/holder
Lamps
Lessons—contribute to
Letter opener

THE LISTS

Liqueurs/Brandy
Mirrors
Mugs
Organizers
Paperweight
Pens, pencils
Photographs
Plants
Posters
Prints
Puzzles
Radio
Rugs
Sculpture
Sleeping bag
Smoking accessories
Stationery
Subscriptions
T-shirt
Tennis items
Thermos decanter
Time, yours
Towels, guest
Travel accessories
Vase
Wastebasket
Wine
Wristwatch

EMOTIONAL/FUN GIFTS
For Friends

Appliances, electric
Artist supplies

Backgammon/board games
Balloons
Bar accessories
Beach items
Bed tray
Belts
Bicycle
Binoculars
Bird feeder
Blazer buttons
Bookends
Bookmarks
Books
Brandy snifters
Bubblebath
Calculator
Calendars
Camera accessories
Candle snuffer
Candy
Cards, playing
Certificates
Chess set
Chocolate
Christmas ornaments
Cigars
Clock
Clothes
Cocktail napkins
Coffee mug
Coffee, teas
Color charting
Computer accessories

- Decanters
- Decorative accessories
- Desk accessories
- Dining accessories
- Door knocker
- Earphones
- Escargot utensils
- Ethnic cuisine cookware
- Evening bag
- Expresso pot
- Facial, manicure, pedicure
- Fireplace accessories
- Flashlight
- Flowers, real/silk
- Food
- Frames
- Globe
- Gloves
- Hair accessories
- Hair appliances
- Hammock
- Handbags
- Hats
- Herbs, spices
- Home-made food
- Humidors
- Hurricane lamps
- Ice cream scoop
- Jewelry
- Jumprope
- Key rack
- Key ring/holder
- Kitchen accessories
- Kitchen appliances
- Kitchen gadgets
- Kites
- Knapsack
- Lamps
- Lessons—contribute to
- Letter opener
- Linens, bed
- Lingerie
- Liqueurs/Brandy
- Magnets
- Massage
- Metronome
- Microscope
- Mirrors
- Mistletoe
- Mobiles
- Models—cars, airplanes
- Movies
- Mugs
- Museum membership
- Napkin rings
- Needlepoint
- Nutcracker
- Nuts, canned
- Opera glasses
- Organizers
- Pajamas
- Paperweight
- Pens, pencils
- Perfume
- Pet accessories
- Phonograph records

The Lists

Photo album
Picnic basket
Plants
Posters
Prints
Puzzles
Radio
Remote control
Robe/dressing gown
Rug
Sachéts
Salad bowl
Scarf
Sculpture
Seeds
Shoe polish kit
Sleeping bag
Slippers
Smoking accessories
Sporting goods, clothes
Stationery
Stuffed animal
Subscriptions
Suspenders
T-shirt
Teapot
Tennis items
Theater tickets
Thermos decanter
Time, yours
Towels, guest
Toys
Travel accessories

Vase
Videocassetes
Wastebasket
Wine
Wine coaster
Wine rack
Wristwatch
Yoyo

EMOTIONAL/FUN GIFTS
For Birthdays

Appliances, electric
Artist supplies
Backgammon/board games
Balloons
Bar accessories
Barometer
Beach items
Bed tray
Belts
Bicycle
Binoculars
Bird feeder
Blazer buttons
Bookends
Bookmarks
Books
Brandy snifters
Bubblebath
Calculator
Calendars
Camera accessories
Candle snuffer

GIFTING RIGHT

Candy
Cards, playing
Certificates
Chess set
Child's dinnerware set
Chinese cookery
Chocolates
Christmas ornaments
Cigars
Clocks
Clothes
Cocktail napkins
Coffee mugs
Coffee, teas
Color charting
Computer accessories
Decanters
Decorative accessories
Desk accessories
Dining accessories
Door knocker
Earphones
Escargot utensils
Evening bag
Expresso pot
Facial, manicure, pedicure
Fireplace accessories
Flashlight
Flowers, real/silk
Food
Frames
Globe
Gloves

Hair accessories
Hair appliances
Hammock
Handbags
Hats
Herbs, spices
Home-made food
Ice cream scoop
Jewelry
Jumprope
Key rack
Key ring/holder
Kitchen accessories
Kitchen appliances
Kitchen gadgets
Kites
Knapsack
Lamps
Lessons—contribute to
Letter opener
Linens, bed
Lingerie
Liqueurs/Brandy
Magnets
Massage
Metronome
Microscope
Microscope
Mirrors
Mistletoe
Mobiles
Models—cars, airplanes
Movies

THE LISTS

Mugs
Museum membership
Napkin rings
Needlepoint
Nutcracker
Nuts, canned
Opera glasses
Organizers
Pajamas
Paperweight
Pens, pencils
Perfume
Pet accessories
Phonograph records
Photo album
Photographs
Picnic basket
Plants
Posters
Prints
Puzzles
Radio
Remote control
Robe/dressing gown
Rug
Sachéts
Scarf
Sculpture
Seeds
Shoe polish kits
Sleeping bag
Slippers
Smoking accessories

Sporting goods, clothes
Stationery
Stuffed animals
Subscriptions
Suspenders
Sweater
T-shirt
Teapot
Telephone
Tennis items
Theater tickets
Thermos decanter
Time, yours
Towels, guest
Toys
Travel accessories
Vase
Videocassetes
Wastebasket
Wine
Wine coaster
Wristwatch
Yoyo

EMOTIONAL/FUN GIFTS
For Office Occasions

Appliances, electric
Barometer
Binoculars
Bookends
Books
Calculator
Camera accessories

Gifting Right

Candy
Chocolates
Clocks
Computer accessories
Desk accessories
Flowers, real/silk
Home-made food
Jewelry
Lamps
Letter opener
Liqueurs/Brandy
Mirrors
Mugs
Organizers
Paperweight
Prints
Rug
Sculpture
Smoking accessories
Stationery
Subscriptions
Thermos decanter
Travel accessories
Vase
Wastebasket

**EMOTIONAL/FUN GIFTS
For Get Well**

Appliances, electric
Artist supplies
Backgammon/board games
Balloons
Bed tray
Bird feeder
Bookends
Bookmarks
Books
Camera accessories
Candy
Cards, playing
Certificates
Chess set
Chocolates
Cocktail napkins
Coffee mugs
Desk accessories
Earphones
Evening bag
Facial, manicure, pedicure
Flowers, real/silk
Food
Frames
Hair accessories
Hair appliances
Hats
Home-made food
Jewelry
Jumprope
Kitchen gadgets
Kites
Lessons—contribute to
Linens, bed
Lingerie
Liqueurs/Brandy
Massage
Mistletoe

The Lists

Mobiles
Models—cars, airplanes
Movies
Mugs
Museum membership
Needlepoint
Opera glasses
Pajamas
Pens, pencils
Perfume
Pet accessories
Phonograph records
Photo album
Photographs
Plants
Posters
Prints
Puzzles
Radio
Remote control
Robe/dressing gown
Scarf
Sculpture
Seeds
Slippers
Stuffed animals
Subscriptions
Suspenders
T-shirt
Teapot
Tennis items
Theater tickets
Thermos decanter
Time, yours
Toys
Travel accessories
Vase
Videocassetes
Yoyo

EMOTIONAL/FUN GIFTS
For Host/Hostess

Appliances, electric
Backgammon/board games
Balloons
Bar accessories
Bookends
Bookmarks
Books
Calendars
Candle snuffer
Candy
Cards, playing
Certificates
Chocolates
Christmas ornaments
Cigars
Cocktail napkins
Coffee mugs
Coffee, teas
Dining accessories
Door knocker
Escargot utensils
Expresso pot
Fireplace accessories
Flowers, real/silk

GIFTING RIGHT

Food
Frames
Herbs, spices
Home-made food
Ice cream scoop
Jewelry
Key rack
Kitchen accessories
Kitchen gadgets
Letter opener
Liqueurs/Brandy
Magnets
Mistletoe
Movies
Mugs
Napkin rings
Nutcracker
Nuts, canned
Paperweight
Perfume
Pet accessories
Phonograph records
Photo album
Photographs
Plants
Posters
Prints
Puzzles
Sachéts
Scarf
Seeds
Smoking accessories
Stationery

Teapot
Theater tickets
Towels, guest
Toys
Travel accessories
Vase
Yoyo

**EMOTIONAL/FUN GIFTS
For Housewarming**

Appliances, electric
Backgammon/board games
Bar accessories
Barometer
Bed tray
Binoculars
Bird feeder
Bookends
Brandy snifters
Bubblebath
Camera accessories
Candy
Certificates
Chinese cookery
Chocolates
Clocks
Cocktail napkins
Coffee mugs
Coffee, teas
Decanters
Decorative accessories
Dining accessories
Escargot utensils

The Lists

Expresso pot
Fireplace accessories
Flashlight
Flowers, real/silk
Food
Globe
Hammock
Herbs, spices
Home-made food
Ice cream scoop
Key rack
Kitchen accessories
Kitchen appliances
Kitchen gadgets
Kites
Lamps
Lessons—contribute to
Letter opener
Linens, bed
Liqueurs/Brandy
Mirrors
Mugs
Napkin rings
Nutcracker
Nuts, canned
Organizers
Photo album
Photographs
Plants
Posters
Prints
Radio
Rug

Salad bowl
Sculpture
Seeds
Sleeping bag
Smoking accessories
Stationery
Subscriptions
Teapot
Telephone
Thermos decanter
Time, yours
Towels, guest
Toys
Vase
Wastebasket
Wine

EMOTIONAL/FUN GIFTS
For Wedding Showers

Appliances, electric
Balloons
Bar accessories
Bed tray
Bookends
Camera accessories
Candle snuffer
Certificates
Chinese cookery
Christmas ornaments
Clocks
Coffee mugs
Dining accessories
Door knocker

Escargot utensils
Flowers, real/silk
Frames
Ice cream scoop
Jewelry
Key rack
Kitchen accessories
Kitchen appliances
Kitchen gadgets
Knives, cheese
Lamps
Letter opener
Linens, bed
Lingerie
Liqueurs/Brandy
Massage
Mirrors
Mugs
Opera glasses
Pajamas
Phonograph records
Photo album
Picnic basket
Prints
Radio
Robe/dressing gown
Salad bowl
Subscriptions
Sweater
Teapot
Telephone
Thermos decanter
Time, yours

Towels, guest
Travel accessories
Vase
Wastebasket
Wine coaster

EMOTIONAL/FUN GIFTS
For Weddings

Appliances, electric
Brandy snifters
Certificates
Clocks
Decanters
Decorative accessories
Dining accessories
Door knocker
Escargot utensils
Flowers, real/silk
Frames
Jewelry
Kitchen appliances
Lamps
Linens, bed
Mirrors
Napkin rings
Prints
Radio
Rug
Salad bowl
Sculpture
Teapot
Telephone
Vase

The Lists

Wastebasket
Wine

**EMOTIONAL/FUN GIFTS
For Second Weddings**

Appliances, electric
Bar accessories
Barometer
Beach items
Bed tray
Binoculars
Bird feeder
Bookends
Brandy snifters
Camera accessories
Candle snuffer
Certificates
Chess set
Chinese cookery
Clocks
Coffee mugs
Decanters
Decorative accessories
Dining accessories
Door knocker
Earphones
Escargot utensils
Expresso pot
Fireplace accessories
Flowers, real/silk
Frames
Globe
Hammock

Jewelry
Kitchen accessories
Kitchen appliances
Lamps
Letter opener
Linens, bed
Lingerie
Liqueurs/Brandy
Mirrors
Napkin rings
Needlepoint
Nutcracker
Opera glasses
Pens, pencils
Photo album
Photographs
Picnic basket
Prints
Radio
Rug
Salad bowl
Sculpture
Smoking accessories
Stationery
Teapot
Telephone
Theater tickets
Thermos decanter
Time, yours
Towels, guest
Travel accessories
Vase
Wastebasket

GIFTING RIGHT

Wine
Wine coaster

**EMOTIONAL/FUN GIFTS
For Baby Showers**

Appliances, electric
Balloons
Bookends
Books
Bubblebath
Certificates
Child's dinnerware set
Clocks
Clothes
Frames
Lamps
Mobiles
Pajamas
Photo album
Posters
Prints
Robe/dressing gown
Rug
Toys
Wastebasket

**EMOTIONAL/FUN GIFTS
For Anniversaries**

Appliances, electric
Backgammon/board games
Bar accessories
Barometer

Bed tray
Binoculars
Bird feeder
Bookends
Books
Calendars
Candle snuffer
Candy
Certificates
Chess set
Chinese cookery
Chocolates
Christmas ornaments
Cigars
Clocks
Decanters
Decorative accessories
Dining accessories
Door knocker
Escargot utensils
Evening bag
Expresso pot
Fireplace accessories
Flowers, real/silk
Frames
Globe
Hammock
Herbs, spices
Home-made food
Jewelry
Kitchen accessories
Kitchen appliances
Kitchen gadgets

The Lists

- Lamps
- Letter opener
- Linens, bed
- Lingerie
- Liqueurs/Brandy
- Mirrors
- Mugs
- Napkin rings
- Nutcracker
- Opera glasses
- Paperweight
- Pens, pencils
- Phonograph records
- Photo album
- Photographs
- Picnic basket
- Plants
- Prints
- Radio
- Robe/dressing gown
- Salad bowl
- Sculpture
- Sleeping bag
- Smoking accessories
- Sporting goods, clothes
- Stationery
- Subscriptions
- Sweater
- Teapot
- Telephone
- Theater tickets
- Thermos decanter
- Time, yours
- Towels, guest
- Travel accessories
- Vase
- Videocassetes
- Wastebasket
- Wine
- Wine coaster
- Wristwatch

FOR PERSONS WITH EVERYTHING

Practical Gifts

Cord of wood with fireplace accessories.

Gift certificate for a custom-made suit or dress.

Designer Umbrellas (initials engraved).

Initialed jewelry (e.g. cuff links).

Silver or Brass luggage tags.

English heated towel stand.

Electric plate warmer.

Jeweler's ultrasonic cleaner .

(The above three items are available at Hammacher Schlemmer. Stores/catalogs such as The Sharper Image also have excellent gifts for the person who has everything).

Contribution in the Giftee's names to a local or national charity.

Gold-plated paperclips (not real gold) for successful executive.

A half dozen sessions with a personal trainer (exercise, dance, sport, etc.) to get someone started.

Custom-made gifts:

Professional photograph—either traditional pose, or a sexy pose if appropriate.

Large leather or vinyl scrapbook with pictures of one's hometown (or other nostalgic location), including letters and pictures from persons significant to Honoree's life. "This is Your Life" scrapbook.

Business card made into a clock.

Investments/Things that grow:

An indoor tree or a tree to plant outside; present it with ceremonial flourish, "The John Smith Memorial tree." Include care and feeding instructions.

A yearly contribution to a mutual fund or stocks and bonds.

Fine vintage wine or brandy.

Work of art or sculpture by an established artist.

Rare stamp or coin.

Aquarium with rare fish.

Exotic plant (e.g. Venus Fly Trap).

"Event" gifts:

Reserve a movie theater or auditorium, serve champagne and popcorn.

Gather 30-50 friends and rent an entire train car and visit a nearby or faraway city for the day, evening, or weekend.

A formal breakfast kidnapping. Call up your birthday friend at the crack of dawn, say he/she has one hour to dress up before their limousine and chauffeur will arrive. Arrange a formal breakfast for 6-8 friends in the garden of a historical mansion, in the center of a public park or indoor courtyard, or on the deck of a ship. (Many tourist spots at 7:30 a.m. are empty and rather magical).

Two tickets to a tropical island for the weekend; include suntan oil and spending money.

The Lists

Arrange to fly an entire family to visit grandparents or other relatives.

Season tickets to a favorite theater, ballet or local sports event.

A ride in a helicopter or hot air balloon.

Tickets to major event (Olympics, Superbowl, World Series, etc.).

Season pass for ski lift tickets.

For those who like to cook and eat:

Basket of ethnic spices or condiments: Chinese, Middle Eastern, Indian, Mexican.

Pastamaker with pasta cookbook or a selection of fresh pasta, sauces and Parmesan.

Expresso/Cappucino machine or other exotic kitchen appliance.

Chocolates in the shape of the person's initials or other shapes, like a tennis racket or woman's leg.

Antique tin container full of gourmet candies.

A Taste of America features a selection of foods from different U.S. regions. Telephone orders 24-hours a day 202/342-5501.

Selection of fine jams, mustards, meats, nuts, fruits or whatever—through mail order catalogs or compiled into a nicely decorated box or reusable container. For some occasions, just one jar of a gourmet food will do.

Light-hearted gifts:

Cartoon or comical slippers or socks for everyone in the family—adults and kids.

Puppets and a puppet theater with scenery. Make it with friends and relatives if you cannot afford them at a toy store.

Cookie-of-the-Month. A tin of cookies are sent monthly to the person of your choice.

Autographed photo or book of favorite star, author or VIP.

Sterling silver toothpaste turner with person's initials (Tiffany & Co.)

Arrange to have an airplane skywrite a personal message.

TITLES BY CCC PUBLICATIONS

—NEW BOOKS—

THE SUPERIOR PERSON'S GUIDE TO EVERYDAY IRRITATIONS
HOW TO TALK YOUR WAY OUT OF A TRAFFIC TICKET
YOUR GUIDE TO CORPORATE SURVIVAL
WHAT DO WE DO NOW?? (The Complete Guide For All New Parents Or Parents-To-Be)

—WINTER 1990 RELEASES—

GIFTING RIGHT (How To Give A Great Gift For Any Occasion Every Time)
HOW TO REALLY PARTY
HORMONES FROM HELL
SINGLE AND AVOIDING AIDS

—BEST SELLERS—

NO HANG-UPS (Funny Answering Machine Messages)
NO HANG-UPS II
NO HANG-UPS III
GETTING EVEN WITH THE ANSWERING MACHINE
HOW TO GET EVEN WITH YOUR EXes
HOW TO SUCCEED IN SINGLES BARS
TOTALLY OUTRAGEOUS BUMPER-SNICKERS
THE "MAGIC BOOKMARK" BOOK COVER [Accessory Item]

—CASSETTES—

NO HANG-UPS TAPES (Funny, Pre-recorded Answering Machine Messages With Hilarious *Sound Effects*)—In Male or Female Voices

Vol. I: GENERAL MESSAGES
Vol. II: BUSINESS MESSAGES
Vol. III: 'R' RATED
Vol. IV: SOUND EFFECTS ONLY

Coming Soon:
Vol. V: CELEBRI-TEASE (Celebrity Impersonations)
Vol. VI: MESSAGES FOR SPORTS FANS